# GHANA @ 60: EVOLUTION OF THE LAW, DEMOCRATIC GOVERNANCE, HUMAN RIGHTS AND FUTURE PROSPECTS

*Proceedings of a Conference,*
*9th-10th March 2017, LBC Auditorium,*
*University of Professional Studies,*
*Accra (UPSA), Ghana*

FRANCISCA KUSI-APPIAH (ED.)

# GHANA @ 60: EVOLUTION OF THE LAW, DEMOCRATIC GOVERNANCE, HUMAN RIGHTS AND FUTURE PROSPECTS

*Proceedings of a Conference, 9th-10th March 2017, LBC Auditorium, University of Professional Studies, Accra (UPSA), Ghana*

GALDA VERLAG 2019

Bibliografische Information der Deutschen Nationalbibliothek
Die Deutsche Nationalbibliothek verzeichnet diese Publikation in der Deutschen
Nationalbibliografie; detaillierte bibliografische Daten sind im Internet über
http://dnb.ddb.de abrufbar.


© 2019 Galda Verlag, Glienicke

**ISBN 978-3-96203-080-3 (Print)**
ISBN 978-3-96203-081-0 (Ebook)

# TABLE OF CONTENTS

### 3 ADJUDICATION OF HUMAN RIGHT CASES BY THE COURTS
Mavis Ekua Enyamah Kwainoe

8 'I AM INDEPENDENT BUT I SPEAK MY MASTER'S TONGUE': A PARADOX OF INDEPENDENCE AND THE NEED TO TRANSLATE THE CONSTITUTION INTO GHANAIAN LANGUAGES
Brian S. Akrong

9 LEGISLATING SUSTAINABLE DEVELOPMENT: GHANA'S PATH TO DEVELOPMENT
Edmund Ato Kwaw & P. Ebow Bondzi-Simpson

# LIST OF CONTRIBUTORS

Atupare Atudiwe P., PhD., Senior Lecturer, Faculty of Law, University of Ghana, Accra, Legon.
   Research Interests: Jurisprudence, Criminal Law, Constitutional Law, Administrative Law, Employment Law, Human Rights, Private International Law, Law of Torts and Legal Ethics

Brian S. Akrong, PhD, Senior Lecturer and Coordinator of Publications, Department of Public Relations, University of Professional Studies, Accra (UPSA)
   Research Interests: English, Law and Public Administration

Edmund Ato Kwaw, D.Jur, Associate Professor of Law & Head of Department, Private Law, Faculty of Law, University of Professional Studies, Accra (UPSA)
   Research Interests: Banking and Finance, Human Rights, International Trade and Investment, Commercial Law and Administrative Law

Francisca Kusi-Appiah, PhD, Acting Head of Department (Public Law), Lecturer and Research Officer, Faculty of Law, University of Professional Studies, Accra (UPSA)
   Research Areas: Laws of Natural Resources, Energy Law, Competition Law, Environmental Law, Law of Contract, Comparative Law and Alternative Dispute Resolution and Sustainable Development

Kwame Frimpong, JSD, Dean & Professor of Law Emeritus, Faculty of Law, University of Professional Studies, Accra (UPSA)
   Research Interests: Law and Accountable Institutions, Criminal Law, Law and Development, Human Rights and International Law.

Lydia A. Nkansah, PhD, Dean and Associate Professor of Law at the Kwame Nkrumah University of Science and Technology (KNUST) in Kumasi, Ghana.
   Research Areas: Human Rights, Constitutional Law, Transitional justice, International criminal justice, Legal jurisprudence and Consumer protection

Maame Efua Addadzi – Koom, LLM, Assistant Lecturer, Faculty of Law, Kwame Nkrumah University of Science and Technology (KNUST) in Kumasi, Ghana.
   Research Areas: Constitutional Law, Human Rights, Comparative Law and Sustainable Development

Mavis Ekua Enyamah Kwainoe, LLM, Lecturer & LLB Programme Coordinator, Faculty of Law, University of Professional Studies, Accra (UPSA)

Research Areas: Human Rights Law, International Law, Criminal Law and Law of Tort

P. Ebow Bondzi-Simpson, S.J.D., Professor of Law, and Rector of the Ghana Institute of Management and Public Administration (GIMPA), Accra.

Research Interests: Human Rights and Humanitarian Law, Public International Law, International Law and Relations, Securities Selling and Investment Advice

Samuel .A. Adjei, Final year Law Student and Former President of the Law Students Union, UPSA.

Research Interests: Law and Accountable Institutions, Criminal Law, Law and Development, Human Rights and International Law.

S.O Gyandoh Jnr., PhD., Professor of Law Emeritus, Temple University School of Law, Philadelphia, U.S.A

Research Interests: Constitutional law, Comparative law, Human Rights and Administrative Law

Thomas Appiah Kubi Asante, Mphil, Assistant Registrar, University of Professional Studies Accra (UPSA)

Research Interests: Teaching and learning, pedagogy and education, teaching, professional development and public administration

$$1$$

# GHANA @ 60: A PERSONAL PERSPECTIVE

## S.O. Gyandoh Jnr.

**Abstract**

The Author gives a concise narrative of the evolution of law since the arrival of the British Colonial Masters in Ghana (formerly known as the Gold Coast). He further adds his personal perspective of the democratic governance and human rights protection in Ghana through the first Republican Government to the Fourth Republic.

**Greetings and Salutations:**

The Diamond Jubilee of any Nation-State presents an occasion that decidedly calls for a pause to reflect on what has gone on before, and then focus on ways to identify and promote preferred and shared national goal values. That is why we owe profound gratitude to the organisers of this two-day conference.

For me personally, the occasion evokes powerful nostalgic memories. Here is why: in 1956, that is, one year before Ghana's Independence from colonial rule, I was one of the last three beneficiaries of the then colonial Government's Scholarship scheme, under which students from the secondary schools of this country were sent abroad to the U.K to study Law, which was not one of the disciplines you could study at the University College of the Gold Coast. As I recall, we flew to London, U.K in an aircraft operated by British Overseas

Airways Corporation (BOAC) - yes quite a mouthful!

Barely a year later, I was one of the students chosen to travel to London from my University base to participate in the celebration of Ghana's Independence at the posh Savoy Hotel on the banks of the River Thames. I was dazzled by the super luxurious appointments of the venue. We were all made to feel very proud that from that date, the 6th of March, 1957, we were to be described as Citizens of Ghana, not subjects of the British Empire.

On the way back, again by train, from the celebrations at Savoy Hotel, I vividly recalled an event that had occurred during my first six months in the U.K. I had been sent to spend a weekend with a British family of Husband, Wife and a daughter of 8-9 years old. They lived in Maidenhead, a picturesque little village. On the evening of my arrival, as we sat in a small hall with BBC radio in the background, the madam of the house (Wife) introduced me as a young man from the Gold Coast colony studying Law at the University of Southampton. As soon as she finished, the young girl of 8 or 9 years old looked intently at her mother and asked "Mother, did you say the Gold Coast? Is that ours?" meaning "is that part of our overseas dominions?" I was utterly flabbergasted at the time. Meanwhile, my passport described me as a subject of British Monarch, who's Empire, however, was only a shadow of its former glory, largely as a result of the devastation of the 2nd World War, and the loss of India and Pakistan in 1947.

On this my train trip back to Southampton, and ever afterwards, I felt, and continue to feel, emancipated, personally, from the burden that had been so dramatically stamped on my consciousness by a little British girl.

Not too long after the celebration in London all of us holding British passports were given the option by the newly-installed Ghana High Commission in London to exchange our colonial passports for newly printed Ghana Passports. It was with much great pride in my heart, speaking for myself, that I took steps to exchange my British passport for that of a Ghanaian citizen.

Madam Chairperson, this two-day Conference, of which I have the honour and privilege of being the keynote speaker, is meant to provide a platform for the discussion of "Issues related to governance, politics and Law within the context of the Fourth Republic", according to the organizers of the Conference.

Notwithstanding the request to centre our attention on the Fourth Republic, which began in January, 1992, I believe it is necessary to sharpen our awareness of some major landmarks in the development of our motherland from colonial times to the present. Such awareness is bound to enrich our understanding of the present constitutional arrangement which informs our modalities of governance. Hopefully, such awareness will also inspire qualitative improvements in the future. For these reasons a few remarks drawing attention to our not-so-distant past-relatively speaking, that is – will, in my humble view, be in order.

## Major Landmarks in the Development of Law in Ghana

So far as the evolution of the law is concerned, the fascinating story of this evolution may conveniently be taken to begin in 1830, i.e. nearly 200 years ago. That was the year when a young British soldier by the name of Captain George Maclean, was sent to the Gold Coast by the British colonial government. He performed his purely administrative duties with such vigor and enthusiasm that he later acted as Governor until his death in 1847, when he was buried at Cape Coast Castle, where his remains still lie.

Captain Maclean was sent to the Gold Coast to take care of the day-to-day management and administration of British forts and settlements on the Gold Coast. At the same time, political responsibility for the government of these forts and settlement was given to a committee of merchants, who had for some time been trading there. His high enthusiasm in the performance of his duties as administrative manager ultimately led to his becoming the first to lay the foundations of British administration of justice in Ghana.

He was indeed appointed judicial assessor and Chief Magistrate in 1843, the same year that his successor as Governor, Commander Hill, was appointed. And, as we all know, it was only a year after Commander Hill had become governor that the famous "Bond of 1844" was signed between himself (representing the British Government) and a few chiefs of the Fanti Coastland in and around Cape Coast in the Central Region.

I must enter an important caveat at this point: In 1944, the centenary year of the Bond of 1844, I was a "standard 4 pupil at Bekwai Methodist School in Ashanti, and there were widespread whisperings among the populace, including pupils of relatively advanced age, to the effect that British White people on the Gold Coast were going to be driven out, if necessary by force, in accordance with the terms of the Bond of 1844. This could lead to a hot war! All this was of course, preposterous rumor-mongering. There was no time-stipulation in the Bond, and, in any case, Ashanti did not officially become part of the Gold Coast Colony's Legislative Council until 1946, as we shall see, so, there was no need for panic.

But the real caveat, for our purposes here this morning, is that the Bond of 1844 had very limited and tightly circumscribed legal scope and effect. Under it, the British Crown was empowered to exercise "judicial power and jurisdiction" for the "the protection of individuals and property" within the coastal territories, acknowledged by all to be under the absolute suzerainty of the indigenous peoples, or Aborigenes to the Bond. As I shall presently show, until July 24, 1874, no foreign power could claim any part of what was to become the Gold Coast Colony, and much later, Ghana, as an Imperial Possession.

For us, the importance of the Bond of 1844 lies in the date and month on which it was signed. These happen to be the same date in 1957 described as "the appointed day" for the coming into force of Ghana's Independence Constitution by an imperial "Order in Council" issuing from "the Court at Buckingham Palace on the 22nd day of February, 1957"

After the Bond of 1844, the next important landmark in the development of the Law, for our purposes here today, is July 24, 1874, which as earlier hinted by me marks the formal beginning of the incorporation of the English Common Law as a basic contextual feature of our Legal System. It is by virtue of this imperial incorporation that we can correctly, speak of Ghana as belonging to the Common Law Tradition of Law, in contradistinction, to the Civil Law Tradition, which is based on Roman law, codified as Corpus Juris Civilis by Emperor Justinian in the 6th Century AD (Circa 528)

As we have seen, the evolution of the Law, as we know it, began informally under Captain Maclean and continued with formal legalization under Commander Hill into the laws of the Gold Coast in 1874. This was quickly followed by the passage of the Supreme Court Ordinance of 1876. This important landmark law established the courts, which would from that time on, administer the laws of the Gold Cost colony.

Now, we can go through a brief survey of the progress we have made so far up to the operation of our present Constitution of the Fourth Republic, 1992 noting our high and low points as a nation along the way.

The Independence Constitution of March 6, 1957 lasted until June 30, 1960 and it did not even pretend to concern itself with anything like the comprehensive protection of Human Rights. Parliament was simply empowered "to make laws for the peace, order and good government of Ghana". The prevailing rule was derived from the Roman maxim: "Ubi jus, ibi remedium": That is to say, one had a remedy at law only where the law created a right to such remedy. Thus, the individual could say what he liked or do what he pleased, except to the extent that the law forbade speech(as in the case of slander or libel)or action (as in the case of nuisance or murder). Under that Constitution, a limited power of judicial review of legislation was granted in three specific cases, where a statute law:

> i. sought to compulsorily acquire property (movable or immovable) without adequate compensation
> ii. sought to discriminate against members of a racial community in the imposition of liabilities
> iii. sought to interfere with a person's freedom of conscience and religion

In all three cases, the Supreme Court was invested with original and exclusive jurisdiction to rule on the validity (or, constitutionality) of such a law when called in question (Sections 31-34, 1957 Constitution.

In practical terms, the independence Constitution was operated as if under it, the Government could "do anything except turn a man into a woman and a woman into a man" as one member of Parliament famously claimed, without acknowledging that the expression had been used earlier vis-à-vis the British parliament, after the constitutional settlement of 1688-9 referred to as the Glorious Revolution.

If the independence Constitution of 1957 made no pretenses to a comprehensive protection of Human Rights, our first home-grown Republican Constitution of 1960 made some pretenses at a general, comprehensive protection of Human Rights. Article 13(1) of that Constitution, as is well known, required our first President to declare that he would adhere to certain "fundamental principles", among which was the following:

> "That subject to such restrictions as may be necessary for preserving public order, morality or health, no person should be deprived of freedom of religion or speech, of the right to move and assemble without hindrance, or of the right of access to courts of law"

It is a notorious fact that in the justly celebrated case of Re Akoto in 1961, the then Supreme Court of this country ruled that the "fundamental principles" merely constituted a political yardstick with which to measure the performance of the President (and his cabinet) and the other political branch of Government, the Parliament (legislative). Thus, in case of any breach, the peoples' remedy is to resort to the ballot box at voting time, not to go to the courts. I do not apologize for stating elsewhere that the Court's ruling in the Akoto case reflected "judicial pusillanimity". Be that as it may, the really notable low of that Constitution against which we should always keep our guard as a nation is to be seen in the constitutional amendments introduced and adopted in 1964. Among other things, those amendments:

> mandated a "national party" designated therein as the " Convention Peoples' Party";

took away the independence of the judiciary with a provision that "the president may at any time for reasons which to him appear sufficient remove from office a judge of the supreme court or a judge of the High Court; changed the colours of the then existing National Flag to those of the Convention Peoples' Party.

The responses to these flagrant attempts to introduce, and in time entrench, a totalitarian regime in Ghana are to be seen in core features of the 2nd, 3rd and 4th Republican Constitutions established in our country in the years 1969, 1979 and 1992 respectively.

The 2$^{nd}$ Republican Constitution of 1969 deliberately set out to combat the excesses of the Executive Authority of the Constitution it replaced. It created a Head of State separate from the Head of Government. The former was a ceremonial President, who, however, had some independent institutions of State, such as the Press (both Video and Printing) placed under his care, to insulate such institutions against Political pressures. The latter was a Prime Minster, who, with his cabinet, ran the day to day affairs of the country. The fragility of this Constitutional arrangement, in operation, made it an easy target of a military coup in less than 3years of its life.

The 3$^{rd}$ Republican Constitution came into force in September, 1979, and was, also, in operation for less than 3 years when it was overthrown by what I call the 2nd coming of J.J.Rawlings - a period which ran from December 1981 to January 1993.

## Military Interventions

Perhaps, here is a good point to pause and take a very brief look at the military interventions in our constitutional governance since independence. The first such intervention was on February 24, 1966 by the combined forces of the military and police. The avowed rationale that was widely publicized was that dictatorship appeared to be the hallmark of the regime, especially after the 1964 Amendments of which mention has been made. The National Liberation Council (as the ousting regime called itself) made it quite clear from the beginning that it was not the business of the military or police to govern and that they had intervened only to nip in the bud an incipient dictatorship which, like Caesars, needed to be stopped in its tracks: As Shakespeare puts it in the mouth of Brutus in Julius Caesar:

"But 'tis a common proof
That lowliness is young ambition's ladder,
Whereto the climber-upward turns his face
But when he once attains the upmost round,
He then unto the ladder turns his back,
Looks in the clouds, scorning the base degrees
By which he did ascend. So Caesar may,
Then, lest he may, prevent."

And so the NLC stands for the "National Liberation Council" struck, and stayed in power, preparing the way for return to civilian rule, under the 2$^{nd}$ Republican constitution.

The next military intervention was ushered in on January 13, 1972 and was first baptized as the National Redemption Council (NRC). In July 1975, the NRC was renamed Supreme Military Council (SMC), but still under the leadership of General Ignatius Kutu Acheampong, who had led the original 13$^{th}$ January coup. Then, suddenly, in July 1978, a palace coup took place within the SMC, and General Acheampong was replaced by General Akuffo, the army Commander at that time, thus, ushering in the regime of SMC II (the second Supreme Military Council),

The penultimate military intervention in this country took place on June 4, 1979. It was also the shortest of military interventions we have had, albeit also the most traumatic in its repercussions. This was the first coming of J.J Rawlings onto our political scene, and the regime that was created was called the Armed Forces Revolutionary Council (AFRC). The AFRC ruled until it handed over power to the government of the third republic in September 1979.

The final military intervention, the Provisional National Defense Council (PNDC), came into force on December 31, 1981 and stayed in power until the coming into force of the Fourth Republican Constitution in January 1993. The leadership of the PNDC was the same as the leadership of the first government formed under the Fourth Republican Constitution. In other words, a military regime, which sometimes called itself "revolutionary", transformed itself into a civilian regime, having submitted itself to democratic processes of elections to both Presidency and Parliament.

A low point in the administration of the PNDC needs to be pointed out, probably as an aberration in our constitutional governance not very dissimilar to the 1964 amendments to our First Republican constitution to which attention has been drawn.

The original Proclamation, which established the PNDC as the government of Ghana was a year later i.e. on the 30th December, 1982 superseded by another Proclamation, which made "supplementary and consequential provisions, compendiously titled PNDC Law 42.

This Law provided, by its Section 63 (3) as follows:

> "Any reference in this law, the proclamation or any other law to "powers of government" shall be construed to include legislative, executive, administrative and judicial powers."

I honestly believe that the emphatic rejection of such a totalitarian conception of governance by the Fourth Republican Constitution augurs well for the good people of Ghana who would never want to be taken away from them the right of access to the law and its processes.

**Concluding Remarks**

Three (3) core values, enshrined in our current 1992 Constitution, and of which we are not prepared to compromise, as shown in our constitutional history (a skeletal outline of which I have just provided) are:

> I. The Supremacy of the Constitution as a fundamental Law of the Land.
> II. The independence of the Judiciary as the final arbiter in all things political.
> III. The total and unconditional rejection and disavowal of military or arbitrary rule.

Of these, the last-mentioned bears repetition by way of some quotes:

Art.3 of the1992 Constitution provides:

"Parliament shall have no power to enact a law establishing one-party state.

Any activity of a person or group of persons which suppresses or seeks to suppress the lawful political activity of any other person or any class of persons, or persons generally is unlawful.

> Any person who-
> by himself or in concert with others by any violent or other unlawful means, suspends or overthrows or abrogates this Constitution or any part of it, or attempts to do any such act; or
> aids and abets in any manner any person referred to in paragraph (a) of this clause:
> commits the offence of high treason and shall, upon conviction, be sentenced to suffer death".

My final submission is that if there are any provisions in our current Constitution which require amendment for optimal operation of the Constitution- and, I am sure there are- the process of amendment should be approached in a national, not a partisan manner. Above all, we should exercise extreme pragmatism of the type supposed to have been exercised by Eve, our first female ancestor, in the Garden of Eden.

The story is told that our first male ancestor, Adam from whose rib Eve was created by God, was in the habit of staying out late in the beautiful fields in and around Eden, sometimes. One night, Adam came back home particularly late, and as he lay down by Eve's side to rest for the remainder of the night, he felt Eve's finger meticulously prying all over his rib cage. After a while, Adam asked Eve, What are you trying to do, keep me awake? "Oh no Eve shot back and then added slowly and deliberately. "I was just counting your ribs to make sure God did not make another woman out of your remaining ribs whom you have been visiting!". What I'm urging on my fellow Ghanaians is that we should adopt the type of quiet pragmatism with which Eve dealt with her feelings of uncertainty and doubt about her soul mate.

**Thank you all very much, and may God bless our homeland Ghana.**

## 2

# THE THEORIES OF STRUCTURAL CONCEPTION OF HUMAN RIGHTS IN GHANA

## Atudiwe P. Atupare

**Abstract**

The protection of human rights can only take place when there is a well defined legal and contitutional framework and efficient institutions that enforce the laws of the country. After independence there have been instances of human rights protection and abuses under both civilian and military regimes. This paper attempts to trace or look at some of the steps of the discourse and experience of human rights in Ghana by examining the theories of the structural conception of human rights, and how such conceptions have informed or otherwise of the historical antecedents of human rights discourse in Ghana and current constitutional framework in respect of the provisions on the fundamental human rights and freedoms in the 1992 Constitution. The Ghanaian human rights legal and constitutional regime sits well with the International Bill of Rights but it does not also reject Afrocentric claims.

## Introduction

It seems reasonable to suggest that both international and domestic law obliges governments to protect their citizens from human rights violations and abuses, and to provide redress for those who suffer such violations and abuses.

Governments also have a duty to combat impunity by, among other measures, imposing sanctions against those who infringe the fundamental human rights of others, and eradicating the conditions that enable and produce the violations and abuses. Throughout the contemporary world, active supreme courts, or constitutional courts and national human rights institutions have emerged as a critical part of the responses of states, especially those undergoing political transition, to serious acts of human rights violations and impunity occasioned by a history of prolonged conflicts and antagonisms. But all this depends on legal or constitutional protections of such rights.

The history and enduring importance of human rights discourse in Ghana, with little or no dispute, takes us back to the dark days of colonial rule – the imposition of foreign political power over natives, and even the Trans-Atlantic Slave trade that every good student of history will know. Acts of dictatorship by the colonial government ensured that the norms of governance were footed on the conception of rule by men or rule by law, not rule of law; and acts of dehumanisation objectified natives and denied them of any propriety of dignity. Since the 18th Century to the first quarter of 1957, substantial actual degradation of human rights as values was a prominent consequence of these two events in the history of Ghana.

But though we still remember and annually celebrate with pride the end of colonial rule and the achievement of independence from British rule on the 6th of March, 1957 under the government of Dr. Kwame Nkrumah, the past and present compass of human rights in this country presents varied and multiple complexions. For instance, we have moments to feel good about human rights and we also have moments to mourn the death of leadership conscience in protecting human rights in Ghana. This ambivalent experience happened under both civilian and military regimes. In this paper, we will attempt to trace or look at some of the steps of the discourse and experience of human rights in Ghana by examining the theories of the structural conception of human rights, and how such conceptions have informed or otherwise of the historical antecedents of human rights discourse in Ghana and current constitutional framework in respect of the provisions on the fundamental human rights and freedoms in the 1992 Constitution.

## Theoretical Conception of the Structure of Human Rights Protection

As the ideas and exposition in this section of the paper may be seem by others as largely situating within the general literature of the rule of law, constitutionalism and human rights in Africa, it is important to briefly capture its specific location and intellectual uniqueness. In fact, there are a number of scholars who have, to their credit, meaningfully attempted answers to the questions about the structure of human rights in a state, how such rights are to be protected and the design of a constitution in protecting such rights. But I confess such responses, as I will show, largely unique and thoughtful with great deal of intellectual vigour, consistency and coherency, failed the somewhat, specific needs of this paper.

Our difference does not only lie in our methodological approach, but also the thematic, juridical and analytical framework. Yet it would seem we are all motivated by the same pains of authoritarianism, misgovernance, military dictatorship, egregious violation of human rights, wars and armed conflicts which have become a conspicuous feature of the world, to seek solution in scholarship. Like these earlier writers, there is appreciably a realisation that prolonged wailings from the bowels of tensed, misruled countries steeped in wars of barbarity, armed conflict, personalisation of state power, authoritarian rule, pervasive corruption and wanton abuse of human rights would do a little to salvage the victims.

This requires a multi-dimensional approach to deal with the problems. This work attempts to describe the theory of the various human rights structure that underlie the constitutional practices of a state in the protection of rights. The theory of a structure of human rights defines the behaviour of a state or the constitutional practice of a state in the protection of rights. This theory might be a function of both the history/culture and political experience of that state. Indeed, of many of the writings on this subject matter, it would seem not necessarily fair, we will identify and categorise three distinct theories or schools of thought. These are the *Evolutionary Theory*, the *Justificatory Theory* and the *Protection and Enforcement Theory*. We shall take these theoretical conceptions one after the other.

### A. The Evolutionary Theory

The evolutionary theory comes from the work of a group of scholars who seek to respond to two interrelated claims: the abrasive claim of Eurocentric writers that indigenous African cultural values or practices are incapable of sustaining a notion of or a concept of human rights, and that human rights are universal. Thus the presumption is that the validity/enforcement of a set of human rights norms does not depend on culture. If such claims are sustained, it appears obvious that Africa and for that matter Ghana not only lacks a recognisable role in the evolutionary history of human rights, but norms of human rights currently found in the Ghanaian constitution must be enforced in accordance with Eurocentric conceptions. The contentious trajectory of such a view may affect a conception of the authority of law fasten to human rights and perhaps the rule of law enforcement in Ghana. The normative questions raised in the ensued contest include: does the cultural normativity of Ghana or Africa provide any justification for the conception of human rights? What is the place of Africa or Ghana as far as the philosophical underpinnings of human rights are concerned? Does African (Ghanaian) philosophy support any conception of human rights independent of Western conceptions?

Reacting to such queries, the evolutionary theory group relied on culture, fundamental values, cosmological ideas, political and social characteristics to demonstrate similarities of human rights norms in Western states and precolonial African societies and states. For instance, Okey Martin Ejidike argues that African fundamental values support the idea of human rights (personhood, dignity, fair trial, human survival etc). Using the history and culture of the Igbo community in Nigeria, Okey found the existence of human rights such as the right to life predicated on cultural prohibition against murder.[1] Needless violence, molestation and killing were thus abhorred as human life was deeply respected.

His account continued that there was a deep rooted cultural and customary injunction against killing of fellow clansman. This was supported by the cosmological ideas held by the Igbo such as a taboo against shedding of human blood regardless of the circumstance, the cultural disapproval of suicide as the corpse of such a person is left unattended, un-mourned and thrown into the evil forest.[2] Such cultural sanctification of life was also among the Dinka of Sudan as Francis Deng suggests that during inter-tribal wars persons outside the battlefield were not to be harmed and victims of famine were entitled to a

---

1 Okey Martin Ejidike, Human Rights in the Cultural Traditions and Social Practice of the Igbo of the South-Eastern Nigeria (1999) 43 Journal of African Law 71. Murder was even remedied in three ways: the perpetrator to take his own life, the gift of a wife to the victim's family and the exiling or banishment of the victim, *ibid* at 76.

2 Okey Martin 77. Consistent with current waves of sexual freedom about same sex marriages, Okey argues Igbo culture allowed marriage between two women, not in response to any homosexual interest, but as a means to cater for barren wealthy women. However, the Nigeria Supreme Court in *Mirebe v. Egwu* (1976) 1 All NLR 266 overruled that custom on the reasoning that it sins against natural justice, equity and good conscience.

relative property as a means to live.[3]

Additionally, the evolutionary theory group also pointed to the cultural recognition of the right of everyone to a tract of land as the beginning of cultural conversation on socio-economic rights among indigenous African societies, namely the Igbo of Nigeria, and the Akan of Ghana as shown by Kwasi Wiredu's account.[4] Land ownership was seen as a means to economic livelihood of the individual and to protect his dignity. It provides shelter and food and consequently bestows a right enforceable on the lineage/ community which has the duty to provide for it upon demand. Problematic though for the Igbo custom (but not the Akan) was the cultural exclusion of women from this benefit of entitlement to land. Igbo patrilineal inheritance system forbids female children from inheriting lands from their parents. This invidious discrimination prompted the Court of Appeal in Nigeria to hold in *Abibatu Folarim v. Flora Cole*[5] that on the death of a founder of a family who has no male child, the eldest daughter should succeed as the head of the family; by implication it includes land and its value to the rights theory under consideration.

Quite apart from these, the existence and protection of human rights like the "right to fair trial" the "right to political participation" and "religious freedom" were also supported by local norms or traditional African political institutions and cultures. On the right to a fair trial, Wiredu asserts that "it was an absolute principle of Akan justice that no human being could be punished without trial".[6] He illustrates this with the trial of a dead person and posthumous punishment symbolically meted out to him if found guilty. Such a trial is particularly, but not exclusively, meticulous, for those who committed suicide in order to evade the consequences of evil conduct. Besides, though religion in the Akan system generally is premised on a belief in and reverence of a Supreme Being, albeit worshipped through ancestors, stools, and gods, Wiredu relies on the phrase, "no one shows God a child" (Obi nykyere akwada Nyame) to suggest that there was no abridgement to religious freedom among the Akan.

3 Francis M. Deng 'A Cultural Approach to Human Rights among the Dinka' in An-Naim & Francis Deng (eds.) *Human Rights in Africa: Cross Cultural Perspectives* (The Brookings Institution, Washington DC, 1990) at 272-3

4 Kwasi Wiredu 'An Akan Perspective on Human Rights' in An-Naim & Francis Deng (eds.) *Human Rights in Africa: Cross Cultural Perspectives* (The Brookings Institution, Washington DC, 1990) at 253-54

5 (1986) 2 NWLR 369

6 Kwasi Wiredu 'An Akan Perspective on Human Rights' at 252

Even sceptics (*ayinyefo*, meant literally, a debater) on secular and non-secular issues exist in the Akan society without any persecution or harm befallen them. Moreover, norms of indigenous political practices and cosmological ideas guarantee participatory rights as the chief could not take decisions without the advice of his councillors and opposition was allowed from the youth, a role spearheaded by the *Nkwakwahene*. Referencing a pre-installation oath from the Ashanti political system the Committee of Experts that drafted the 1992 Ghana's Constitution suggests that civil and political rights such as limited government were known among the Ashanti. The elected chiefs recite as follows:

> We do not want you to abuse us. We do not want you to be miserly; we do not want one who disregards advice; we do not want you to regard us as fools; we do not want autocratic ways; we do not want bullying; we do not like beating. Take the Stool. We bless the Stool and give it to you. The Elders say they give the Stool to you". It would seem from the oath that authoritarian tendencies were to be eschewed, as the elected chief was being told to listen to advice and recognise the participatory rights of the people, who must not be regarded as fools.[7] Ostensibly, decisions were not to be by personal fiat, but consensus. Kwasi Wiredu articulates this as "the right of the people, including the elders, to dismiss a chief who tried to be oppressive"[8]

Be this as it may, it would seem critical that all of such unremitting claims of a cultural basis for the concept of human rights are further troubled by the Eurocentric assertions that what pertains to African is nothing but communitarian sentiments that entitle the individual to some benefits of dignity, not rights. In effect, claims of cultural support of a notion of human rights in Africa do not completely set the evolutionary group free from further engagement as to the universalist assertion that human rights are universal and need not pass a cultural test.

Leading the attack, Jack Donnelly reasons that the concept of human rights cannot be supported in traditional African societies. Non-Western cultural

---

7 To this list of rights backed local norms, Hurst Hannum added the right to education, freedom of movement and a right to work. Hurst Hannum, The Butare Colloquium on Human Rights and Economic Development in Francophone Africa: A Summary and Analysis (1979) 1 Universal Human Rights at 64
8 Kwasi Wiredu 'An Akan Perspective on Human Rights' at 251

and political traditions lack not only the practice of human rights but the very concept, and as a matter of historical fact, the concept of human rights is an artefact of Western civilisation.[9] Thus practices and local norms relied upon by Afrocentrics to make deductions about a conception of human rights are speculative, inconclusive, nebulous and can at best support some notions of human dignity. Donnelly concludes that the concept of human rights is predicated on one's inherent humanity, not one's community ties.

Consistent with this line of reasoning, Bassam Tibi[10] draws a distinction, as it is the case in Rhoda Howard's thesis,[11] between human rights and human dignity and cautions that the two concepts should not be fussed as to suggest that they carry an analogous content. Rhoda Howard pursues this further to propose that human dignity which is an expression of the really moral worth of the individual in relation to society can find easy protection in a society not founded on rights. Louis Henkin records the universal validity of human rights[13], but flatly rejects cultural relativism or what M. Mutua termed multicultural approach to the human rights discourse.[14] He argues that any cultural independence in the construction of human rights is fatal as it will dilute the universal norms enunciated in the Universal Declaration of Human Rights.

Forceful as these Eurocentric claims may seem, they record strong rebuttals from the cultural relativists or the evolutionary theory group. In fact, the Universalists claims of communitarianism and confusion of humanity dignity with human rights have been viewed as either a deliberate misreading of the communitarian thesis or deficient findings as to the African cultural attitude to human rights. Founding their claims, in part, on the conception of man in

9 Jack Donnelly, Human Rights and Human Dignity: An Analytic Critique of Non-Western Conceptions of Human Rights (1982) 76 America Political Science Review 303

10 Bassam Tibi, 'The European Conception of Human Rights and the Culture of Islam' In An-Naim & Francis Deng (eds.) *Human Rights in Africa: Cross Cultural Perspectives*( The Brookings Institution, Washington DC, 1990) at 104-132. Not denying the existence of a notion of human dignity among non-Western cultures such as Africa, Bassam claims the same conclusion cannot be reached for human rights which he considers a contemporary expression of legal entitlements enforceable at the instance of the individual against the State.

11 Rhoda Howard, 'Group versus Individual Dignity in the African Debate on Human Rights' in An-Naim & Francis Deng (eds.) *Human Rights in Africa: Cross Cultural Perspectives* (The Brookings Institution, Washington DC, 1990) at 159-183.

12 Rhoda Howard, 'Group versus Individual Dignity in the African Debate on Human Rights' at pp.119

13 Louis Henkin *The Age of Rights*, (Columbia University Press, 1990) at 17-19

14 Makau Mutua, *Human Rights: A Political and Cultural Critique* (2002) at 58

the African society, Obinna B. Okere observes that "[T]he African conception of a man is not that of an isolated and abstract individual, but an integral member of a group animated by a spirit of solidarity". Kwame Gyekye charges that the fact that the individual's needs and benefits are determined by ties to the community does not in and of itself qualify a suggestion that the African concept of human rights is antithetical to individualism. For him, it merely illustrates the "limited character of the possibilities of the individual" in meeting his basic needs.[15] Makau Mutua has been lucid with a bold expression of this view. He writes:

> "...the concept of the group-centered individual in Africa delicately entwines rights and duties and harmonises the individual with the society. Such a conception does not necessarily see society – organised either as community or the state – as the individual's primary antagonist. Nor does it permit the over-indulgence of the individual at the expense of the society. This conception resists casting the individual as the center of moral universe; instead, both the community and the individual occupy an equally hallowed plane"[16].

It would thus seem that the pursuit of human dignity and rights is not concerned with vindicating the right of any individual against the world. The African notion of family seeks a vindication of communal well-being and that the starting point is not the individual but the whole group including both the living and the dead[17]. The incessant emphasis on community rights does not necessarily antagonise the individual rights as the Eurocentrics claim nor does it permit the over-indulgence of the individual at the expense of the society.[18]

However, a better and more refined defence of this proposition lies with those who argue that the conception of human rights exclusive of the

15 Kwame Gyekye, An Essay on African Philosophical Thought: The Akan Conceptual Scheme (Cambridge University Press, 1987) at 154. He writes: "Communalism may be defined as the doctrine that the group (that is, the society) constitutes the focus of the activities of the individual members of the society. The doctrine places emphasis on the activity and success of the wider society rather than, though not necessarily at the expense of, or to the detriment of, the individual". Ibid at 154

16 Makau Mutua, Human Rights: A Political and Cultural Critique at 65

17 Josiah Cobbah, African values and the human rights debate (1987) 9 Human Rights Q. 321

18 Makau Mutua, Human Rights: A Political and Cultural Critique 65

culture or cosmological ideas of Africa is neither individualistic nor purely communitarian.[19] This argument plies the middle road between the Western conceptions of human rights which recognises the individual as the nucleus of analysis and the cultural relativist Afrocentrics (the hard core of evolutionary theory group) who predicate the concept of human rights on the community. For this group, which is a soft version of the evolutionary theory camp, an African conception of human rights recognises, but does not over-emphasis the community as many writers seem to suggest and strikes a balance between the individual and communal rights.[20] While a communitarian concept of human rights exists in African, it does little to dissuade the thinking that the exercise of such rights is primarily based on the individual.[21] There is therefore an organic nexus between the communal and individual rights.

Perhaps the entire corpus of this human rights debate may still be out there. But it is reasonable to suggest that the Universalists claims may have been incautious. There may have been variations occasioned by different cultural orientations and cosmological ideas between Africa and the West as to the nature and content of these rights, but it is a crude case to make that the cultural practices and traditions that pertained to Africa cannot support a notion of human rights. Besides, seeking a cross-cultural discourse in the human rights debate in and of itself is not a denial of universality of norms of rights. Mutua correctly wrote that "the imposition of the current dogma of human rights on non-European societies flies in the face of the conception of human dignity, and rejects the contributions of other cultures in efforts to create universal corpus of human rights".[22]

To promote human dignity through societal structures, Mutua cautions that there is the need for the human rights constituency to accept cultural pluralism in the debate as a reliable means to establishing a common universal basis for it.[23] An open cultural negotiation on the normative content of human rights law is thus apt. Closing the doors on some cultures not only estranges them but creates some kind of cultural hierarchy that glorifies and celebrates Western culture and denigrates any other cultures. Cross cultural dialogue is thus *sine qua non* to creating a multicultural human rights corpus and to destroy the binary view of the West and the rest of the world on human rights

19 El-Obaid Ahmed El-Obaid and Kwadwo Appiagyei-Atua, Human Rights in Africa: A New Perspective in linking the past to the present (1996) 41 McGill Law Journal 819
20 Ibid at pp.853
21 Ibid at pp.853
22 Makau Mutua, *Human Rights: A Political and Cultural Critique* (2002)at 8
23 Ibid at 9

conceptions, a position which he terms as "a child-parent relationship"

The fruit of this debate however, seems to be limited as far as the specific case of constitutional protection of human rights in Ghana and African in general is concerned. There are still many questions than answers, a state of affairs which requires further probes. In fact, one enduring question is whether the Universalist or Relativist camp prevails, why must the continent largely continue to ignore these human rights norms both sides seem to be extolling? Whether or not there is an African conception of human rights as they exist in current international human rights instruments, it remains as part of constitutional protection of human rights, a goal for African governments to conduct themselves in a clear conformity with these standards.

The continent remains firmly griped by poverty, diseases, especially HIV/AIDS and malaria, and food crises. Democratic governments are frequently interrupted by coup d' etats, armed conflicts and constitutions annulled without remorse. Since independence, majority of African countries have travelled down the shameful road of one-party authoritarian rule, constitutional or military dictatorship, misgovernance, corruption and brutality of civilian population. If the very concept of legal protection of human rights assumes and presupposes the existence of a state that accepts responsibility for upholding the authority of human rights and has the institutional capacity and political will to effect such protection[24], it would seem that the states in Africa, and as the history of Ghana will show, are failing in that role. In short, the state in Africa is or may still be a predator to and devours and imperils human freedom.

### B. Justificatory Theory

It is the weight of these concerns that ignited the scholars under the *Justificatory Theory* to seek answers. The question is fairly asked: Are there peculiar political circumstances in the history of a state or Africa that nurtures or justifies such violations of human rights? On the part of Africa, it has been suggested that the violations are necessary and permissible as a measure of nation building after a rancorous battle for political independence and to foster unity after independence –to end deep cultural and ethnic divisions. Besides, some blame the violations on negative traditional cultural practices

24 Abdullahi Ahmed An-Na'im, 'Introduction: expanding legal protection of human rights in African contexts' in Abdullahi Ahmed An-Na'im (edt) *Human Rights Under African Constitutions: Realising the Promise for Ourselves* (University of Pennsylvania Press, 2002) at pp.4

while others suggest that colonialism is culpable for the violations as it left behind authoritarian political structures and immediate post-independence leaders were steeped in the abusive culture left by such authoritarian political structures. In particular, Abdullahi Ahmed An-Naʿim explains that:

> "It is unrealistic to expect the postcolonial African State to effectively protect human rights when it is the product of colonial rule that is by definition the negation of these rights. However one evaluates precolonial African political regimes from the point of view of human rights, it is clear that colonialism was incapable of creating and sustaining the institutions and processes necessary to protect rights"[25]

The argument here is not that the writers under this rubric condone and endorse the violations, far from that, though it may seem the case for those justifying the violations on the necessity of nation building and national unity. Overbalancing human rights with the interest, however compelling, of nation building may be problematic, especially when human life is involved. It is hardly permissible to wantonly destroy or ostensibly treat with contempt human life as a measure of inducing national unity.

Yet the claims as to the negative effects of colonialism on human rights violation remain unaffected and persuasive. Chidi Anselm Odinkalu suggests a solution in the declaration that "effective protection of human rights in post-independence Africa necessitated a re-orientation of the post-independence African State away from the institutional infrastructure and attitudinal orientation inherited from the colonial period".[26] For him, it is imperative African states reorder their priorities for the human rights project away from mere reporting violations with the sole view of anticipating and preventing them. To this end, Chidi thinks that state building and the construction of civic citizenship allied to education will put the people on a pedestal suitable to hold their governments accountable for human rights violation[27]. Finally,

---

25 Abdullahi Ahmed An-Naʿim "The legal protection of human rights in Africa: how to do more with less" in A. Sara and T.R. Kearns (eds) *Human Rights: Concepts, Contests, Contingencies* 2001, at 89)
26 Chidi Anselm Odinkalu Back to the future: the imperative of prioritising for the protection of human rights in Africa (2003) 47 Journal of African Law 1 at 2
27 Ibid at 4

he argues that partnership between government and civil society in a context of nation building is the only realistic way to generate a better outcome with the human rights project.

But he ends by suggesting as a point of finality a more troubling theory fastened to the contention that there should be a "norm of law that requires government to be constituted by and enjoys some form of electoral legitimacy"[28]. It would seem that the oppressive premise of democratic majority in Africa created misery for the vulnerable and empowered a few elites to impoverish nations and disregard constitutionally protected rights. Increasing claims of tribal and ethnic allegiance to political parties during elections make it difficult to be conclusive on the values of electoral legitimacy in Africa *vis-à-vis* an encompassing national project of re-ordering the priorities of human rights protection. We may thus go beyond electoral legitimacy as a means, not an end, in post-independence campaign for human rights protection in Africa as component of constitutional protection of human rights.

### C. *The protection and Enforcement Theory*

Nevertheless, it remains awkward to justify human rights violations on problematic grounds or merely explain why they are violated using contested reasons which neither provide any convincing answer to the post-war global human rights constituency nor quench the thirst of those seeking constitutional protection of human rights for the much bruised people of Africa. There is an insatiable legitimate interest to look further for ideas and solutions. The *protection and enforcement theory group* assumes this responsibility. Instead of rationalising the violations as the justificatory theory camp did, they begin to examine domestic and regional institutions for failures and solutions.

For instance, what role should human rights Non-Governmental Organisations (NGOs) play in the advancement of human rights and what accounted for judicial failures in the enforcement of fundamental human rights in Africa? What value does regional human rights institutions in Africa add to the human rights and rule of law project[29] and how are such institutions parts of the story of constitutional protection of human rights

---

28 Ibid at 4

29 See a fascinating study by Obiora C. Okafor, *The African Human Rights System: Activist Forces and International Institutions* (Cambridge University Press, 2007)

for the people? In this regard, content and structure of constitutions are studied[30] and more specifically human rights under African constitutions are examined.[31] Attempts are also made to address the interrelatedness of human rights, the rule of law and development[32] and series of writings are produced on the specific value of constitutional democracy[33] in Africa with a specific recourse to human right values upheld in constitutions,[34] good governance,[35] gender equality, affirmative action,[36] electoral legitimacy,[37] minority rights[38] and the role of the media[39].

Answers to these concerns nonetheless varied. On the courts in particular, failures are attributed sharply albeit correctly to corruption, lack of judicial independence, poor infrastructure, political interference, poor public perception, lack of continuing legal education, and judicial conservatism.[40] This is exacerbated by military adventurism and non-ratification of

30 Ben Nwabueze, *The Presidential Constitution of Nigeria*; Leslie Rubin & Pauli Murray, *The Constitution and Government of Ghana* (London: Sweet & Maxwell, African Universities Press, 1964); Oluwole Idowu Odumosu, The Nigeria Constitution: History and Development (London: Sweet & Maxwell, African Universities Press, 1963)

31 Abdullahi Ahmed An-Na'im (edt) *Human Rights Under African Constitutions: Realising the Promise for Ourselves* (University of Pennsylvania Press, 2002)

32 Paul Tiyambe Zeleza & and Philip J. McConnaughay (ed.) *Human Rights, the Rule of Law, and Development in Africa* (Philadelphia: University of Pennsylvania Press, 2004); Claude E. Welch Jr. & Ronald I. Meltzer, *Human Rights and Development in Africa* (Albany: State University of New York Press, 1984)

33 Ben Nwabueze, *Constitutional Democracy in Africa*. Vol. 1-5 (Spectrum Books, 2001)

34 Abdullahi Ahmed An-Na'im (edt) *Human Rights Under African Constitutions: Realising the Promise for Ourselves*

35 Abdalla Bujra & Said Adejumobi, *Breaking Barriers, Creating New Hopes: Democracy, Civil Society, and Good Governance in Africa* (Africa World Press, 2004); Ann Willcox Seidman et al., *Africa's Challenge: Using Law for Good Governance And Development* (Africa World Press, 2007)

36 Adams C., *Affirmative Action in a Democratic Africa*, (Juta Academic, 1993)

37 Staffan Lindberg, The Democratic Qualities of Competitive Elections: Participation, Competition and Legitimacy in Africa (2003) 41 Commonwealth & Comparative Politics 61

38 Appiagyei-Atua, Kwadwo, Minority Rights, Democracy and Development: The African Experience (2008) 15 International Journal on Minority and Group Rights 489

39 Clement E. Asante, *The Press in Ghana: Problems and Prospects* (University Press of America, 1996); Bourgault, Louise M., *Mass Media in Sub-Saharan Africa*, (Indiana University Press, 1995)

40 Okechukwu Oko, Seeking Justice in Transitional Societies: An Analysis of the Problems and Failures of the Judiciary in Nigeria (2005) 31 Brook Journal of International Law 9

international human rights instruments.[41] A classic example from Nigeria on the effects of military governance on the judiciary is in the appeal case of *Nwosu v Environmental Sanitation Authority*[42], where a justice of the Supreme Court openly advised victims of human rights violations to seek a remedy from a different forum, as the Military was clear about the inviolability of its decrees. Such an apologia was premised on the frustrations and contemptuous treatment that the courts have had from the Military with regard to the enforcement of judicial decisions.[43]

But the big gap that remains in all of these studies is how legal theory can be explored as a means to dealing with the serious problems encountered relative to enforcing human rights protected by constitutions in Africa. How can legal theory provide a save valve for the courts in enforcing the constitutions as laws protecting human rights in young democracies like Ghana? Though these questions are explored or addressed elsewhere,[44] this paper falls within an aspect of the protection and enforcement theory camp. An attempt is made here to help the student of human rights in Ghana to understand the 1992 Constitution of Ghana in respect of the provisions protecting the fundamental rights and freedoms. Perhaps future research can engage these theoretical conceptions and their practical bearing to the current Ghana's legal system.

### Historical Context of Human Rights Discourse in Ghana

But before we take a look at how and which rights are protected under the 1992 Constitution, it is helpful to look back into some of the historical antecedents that might form the basis of human rights agitation in this country. In that sense, we may say that human rights discourse in Ghana dates back to the "inglorious" days of colonialism[45] – the imposition of foreign

41 Focusing in part on the role of the judiciary to the protection of human rights in Ghana, Nana K.A. Busia, Jr. stated that "The long periods of military rule have negatively affected the healthy evolution of constitutional jurisprudence, including the interpretation of constitutional provisions on human rights". Nana K.A. Busia, Jr. 'Ghana: Competing Visions of Liberal Democracy' in Abdullahi Ahmed An-Na'im (edt) *Human Rights Under African Constitutions: Realising the Promise for Ourselves* at pp 59 Press, 2007)

42 [1990] 2 NWRL 135 at 688

43 Hakeem O. Yusuf, The Judiciary and Constitutionalism in Transitions: A Critique (2007) 7 Global Jurist 1 at 11

44 Atupare Atudiwe, *Constitutional Justice In Africa: An Examination of Constitutional Positivism, Fundamental Law in Ghana and Nigeria* (South Africa LexisNexis, Butterworth, 2013)[forthcoming]

political power over natives, and the Trans-Atlantic Slave trade.[46] These two events depict the brute aspect of man.[47] The forces of colonialism require that political authority albeit foreign - was never to be questioned. Its aim: to create an atmosphere that was conducive for economic exploitation of the colonies. The slave trade on the other hand commodifies human beings. Accordingly, people were exported to plantation farms in the New World to be used as labour.[48] Today, the "Gates of No Return" in Cape Coast Castle, the first center of political power of colonial Ghana, provide a crude illustration and bitter memories of the sad exit of many young men and women to the New World. They exemplify the possible death of human conscience. One cannot escape a sharp spark of mental pain upon a visit to these sites. If there is ever an injustice to mankind, colonialism and slave trade aptly epitomize its breadth. They represent indignity and injustice, and engender righteous anger in the victims.[49]

While slave trade was formally abolished in the late 18th Century,[50] the struggle to end colonialism lingered on until the second half of the 20th Century. It was the latter that heightens the concerns for human rights in Ghana. The natives legitimately agitated for the respect of human dignity and recognition, values that colonialism had failed to hold as sacrosanct. They sought a complete political independence from the colonialists. The contest was not easy. It was partly civil and partly violence. This produces varied results. Destruction of property and lives was inevitable. But the most celebrated one was the attainment of independence. It became a source of hope and joy to the natives. Hopefully, it signals the end of indignity, political subjugation and economic exploitation.

45 Inglorious, yet some have argued in favor of colonialism that it was for the good of Africa. To them, colonialism has had positive effects for the continent and Ghana for that matter. For instance see L.H. Gann and P. Duignan, *Burden of Empire: An Appraisal of Western Colonialism in African South of the Sahara* (London: Pall Mall, 1968); and, David K. Fieldhouse, "The Economic Exploitation of Africa: Some British and French Comparisons," in P. Gifford and W. Lewis, eds., France and Britain in Africa: Imperial Rivalry and Colonial Rule (New Haven, Conn.: Yale University Press, 1971) 593.

46 For insightful academic commentary on this see Walter Rodney, How Europe Underdeveloped Africa (London: Bougle-L'Ouverture Publications, 1978); and J.D. Anderson, *West and East Africa in the Nineteenth Century* (London: Heinemann, 1972).

47 See Timothy, Fernyhough, "Human Rights and Pre-colonial Africa" in *Human Rights and Governance in Africa* (edt.) Jan Berting et al.( Westport, Conn.: Meckler, 1993)

48 Walter Rodney, *How Europe Underdeveloped Africa*, at pp.534.

49 *ibid*

50 See Suzanne, Miers, *Slavery in the Twentieth Century: The Evolution of a Global Pattern*, (Walnut Creek, CA: AltaMira Press, 2003)

Ghana, as a modern state in the Westphalia[51] sense, achieved independence from British colonial rule on the 6th of March, 1957 under the government of Dr. Kwame Nrumah. Nonetheless, this was not a complete political freedom as expected. The 1957 Independence Constitution provides that Ghana remains a part of the British Empire.[52] By that the laws and government of Ghana were still formally subject to the British Crown. In fact, Ghana's final court of appeal until July 1, 1960 remained the Judicial Committee of the British Privy Council. It could functionally invalidate any Ghanaian law that contradicts British law. Interpretations of the Judicial Committee, even of Ghanaian law, were final and authoritative.[53] This legal institutional linkage may justifiably be conceived as half victory. It allows the shadow of colonialism to loiter around. To some it may be a deception with the view to cool down tempers. Others thought it a big betrayal by the political leaders.[54]

Perhaps it could be argued for the political leaders that half a loaf was better than none. But whether or not these concerns were properly conceived, it makes sense to be sympathetic to their claimants. Complete independence was the desirable end.[55] These apprehensions ignited a renewed determination in the political leaders for constitutional reforms. Their principal demand, at this time, was a republican status. This was granted by the British government on the 1st of July, 1960 with a new constitution. At the most basic level, the 1960 First Republican Constitution, marked Ghana's final step of independence from Great Britain and rejection of the colonial notion of parliamentary sovereignty. It provides the official exit for the graceful departure of Lord Listwell, the then Governor-General who represented the Queen of Britain as a Head of State.

But the immediate post-independence Ghana was not better. Apart from the immediate political benefits of self-governance, the citizens did not get the

---

51 The Treaty of Westphalia was signed in 1648, which brought to an end the Eighty Years' War between Spain and the Dutch and the German phase of the Thirty Years' War. It also marks the birth of Modern State (sovereign and independent state)

52 See Bennion, F.A.R., *The Constitutional Law of Ghana*, (London: Butterworths, 1962) and Rubin, Leslie, *The Constitution and Government of Ghana*, ( London: Sweet & Maxwell Ltd., 1961)

53 *Ibid*

54 For a better opposing arguments on these charges see Toyin, Falola, (edt.), *The Dark Webs: Perspectives on Colonialism in Africa*, ( Durham, N.C. : Carolina Academic Press, 2005)

55 It was better to see off the evil of colonialism than to pretend to do so.

open political space as promised.[56] Political opponents were thrown into jails.[57] Laws were enacted to keep opposition at bay.[58] Worst of all, by a Parliamentary resolution and backed by a referendum, Ghana went back to a de jure one party state. Lamentably, the precious chapter of multi-party constitutional democracy was closed. The value of pluralistic political participation was deeply paled and the sight of salvation seems very far from the people.[59] One party state makes it so. This background may have occasioned the intervention of the military on the 24th February, 1966. This ends the life of the First Republic and the 1960 Constitution. The 1969 and 1979 Constitutions of the Second and Third Republics respectively, ended on a similar note - military takeover, though with an admixture of similar and different reasons.

The longest of these military governments was the eleven-year reign of the Provisional National Defence Council (PNDC).[60] This regime is crucial to our discussion in many respects. In part, it shamefully overthrew the legitimate constitutional government of the third republic.[61] It suspended the 1979 Constitution, declared parliament unlawful to operate and dismissed all ministers from office. Indeed, the government in power prior to the military takeover was effectively disbanded. The regime then ruled with an iron fist

56 Issa Shivji, observes, "For by definition, the neo-colonial state has tended, for its own reproduction, to usurp and obliterate the autonomy of civil society and therefore the very foundation of democracy. It is within this formation that rights struggles, like other democratic struggles, have to be waged." Issue Shivji, *The Concept of Human Rights in Africa* (London: CODESRIA, 1989) at pp.5.

57 Prominent opposition politicians even died in detention cells eg. O. Lamptey and Dr. J.B. Danquah died in Nsawam Prison in 1963 and 1965 respectively

58 The famous one being the *Preventive Detention Act, 1958* which was passed within 24 hours and gave the President the power to cause to be detained without trial any person within the territory of Ghana whom he has reasonable grounds to believe that such a person is causing or likely to cause public disorder. Again, in 1964, there were two major constitutional changes that finally strangled the opposition: A referendum which only allows the introduction of a de jure one-party state and gives the president the power to dismiss any judge on his own reasons.

59 See Afrifa, Amankwa A. The Ghana Coup, (London: Frank Cass, 1966).

60 The PNDC government came to power on 31 December 1981, overthrowing the constitutionally-elected government of Hilla Limann, and ruled the country until January 1992.

61 Though unconvincing, the coup makers cited corruption, economic mismanagement among others as the justification the overthrow of the government.

and gained notoriety for human rights abuses.[62] There were countless tortures, harassments, killings, abductions and disappearances of mostly actual and imagined opponents of the regime.[63] All this happened within the context of an admixture of economic success, decadence and social suffering.[64] In 1992, the PNDC government bowed to a combined force of domestic and international pressures to return the country to a democracy. The regime initiated, guided and supervised the drafting and adoption of *Ghana's Fourth Republican Constitution, 1992*. It must be noted that though this constitution is a direct product of PNDC military politics, it is said to have contained the most elaborate human rights provisions since independence, though it would seem to have taken an inspiration from both the 1969 and 1979 Constitutions and the human rights provisions in those constitutions.

## The 1992 Constitution and Human Rights

From colonialism, slave trade to military dictatorship, the framers of the Fourth Republican Constitution, 1992 were very much aware of the significance of human rights protection. History was a useful guide to them. It was inevitable that this background would influence their deliberation on the nature and future of human rights in Ghana. The preamble of the constitution provides a clear illustration of their vision. In part it states:

62 Among the methods employed by the regime as a mechanism of control are torture, solitary confinement, detention in very dark cells, application of cigarettes to the male organs, mock executions, denial of medical facilities, assault and battery, stripping and denial of legal representation and visits from family. Amnesty International Report on Ghana 20(18 December, 1991) at pp. 20. But note that some writers seem to suggest that human rights violation under Rawling's PNDC was justified. For instance, Jeff Haynes appears to suggest that the violations were necessary in order to protect "collective rights" as opposed to the individual rights advanced by the opponents of the regime. Jeff Haynes, Human Rights and Democracy in Ghana: The Records of the Rawlings Regime (1991) 90 African Affairs 407.

63 Mike, Oquaye, "Human Rights and the Transition to Democracy Under the PNDC in Ghana" (1995) 17 Human Rights Quarterly 556 at p.559

64 See John, Loxley, Ghana: Economic Crisis and the Long Road to Recovery (Ottawa, Canada: North-South Institute, 1988) and Donald, Rothchild, etd., Ghana: the Political Economy of Recovery,(Rienner Publishers, 1991). However, it could be said that the regime was not the worse in Ghana's history in terms of economic woes. Towards the end of the 1980s and early 1990s the regime had been able to sustain a relatively thriving economy through IMF-World Bank backed Structural Adjustment Programme. See John Rapley, Understanding Development: Theory and Practice in the Third World (3rd. Ed) (Lynne Rienner Publishers, 2007)

> We the People of Ghana, in exercise of our natural and inalienable
> right to establish a framework of government which shall secure
> for ourselves and posterity the blessings of liberty, equality of
> opportunity and prosperity,...and in solemn declaration and
> affirmation of our commitment to;...the protection and preservation
> of Fundamental Human Rights and Freedoms, Unity and Stability
> for our nation; enact and give to ourselves this constitution"[65]

Embedded in these words are the values underpinning human rights. Liberty, equality and prosperity represent their concerns for human dignity and the wellbeing of the people. Most importantly, they are anchored by an explicit mention of fundamental human rights and freedoms. These shall be the priority goals of governments. It should be observed that the preamble provides a double intent. Thus, these interests or values must be protected for the present and for posterity. But as the words of the preamble may carry little wait in constitutional interpretation; the framers of the constitution backed them up with elaborate but entrenched provisions on human rights.

Admittedly, it is these provisions that shall provide the general context for this work and how they fit into the *protection and Enforcement Theory* illustrated above. I shall set out these provisions under four distinct headings. Note however that with the exception of the 1960 Constitution which does not contain any open and independent human rights provisions, the current constitutional provisions on human rights are a reproduction of those contained in both the 1969 and 1979 Constitutions. The difference however is in their elaboration in the current Constitution and remarkable additions of such provisions as on Women, Children, Disability and Socio-Economic rights. Therefore, it is not too necessary to recount the provisions of each of these Constitutions here. It suffices to capture the Human Rights provisions in the 1992 Constitution of Ghana.

### Civil and Political Rights

The 1992 Constitution generously replicates the provisions of the Universal Declaration of Human Rights (UDHR) and International Covenant on Civil

---

65 The Preamble, the 1992 Constitution of the Republic of Ghana
66 Smith Rhona K.M., *Textbook on International Human Rights*, (Oxford University Press, 2007) at pp.194
67 UN Human Rights Committee General Comment 6

and Political Rights (ICCPR). These are set out in Chapter 5 of the Constitution. To begin with, the right to life is undoubtedly the most fundamental of all rights. Indeed, all other rights add quality to the life in question and depend on the pre-existence of life itself for their utility.[66] It has been referred to as "the supreme right from which no derogation is permitted even in time of Public emergency."[67] It is also accorded the highest position by those arguing in favour of a hierarchy of rights. Even those not submitting to the hierarchy of rights argument but are generally arguing for a universal fundamentality still consider the right to life one of pre-eminent to which violations can never be remedied.[68] This significant right is provided for in Article 13 of Ghana's Constitution. It states:

> "No person shall be deprived of his life intentionally except in the exercise of the execution of a sentence of a court in respect of a criminal offence under the laws of Ghana of which he has been convicted."[69]

But like other liberal constitutions around the world, a person shall not be held to have deprived another person of his or her life in contravention of this article if that other person dies as a result of a lawful act of war or if that other person dies as a result of the use of force to such an extent as is reasonably justifiable in particular circumstances as- (a) for the defence of any person from violence or for the defence of property; or (b) in order to effect a lawful arrest or to prevent the escape of a person lawfully detained; or (c) for the purposes of suppressing a riot, insurrection or mutiny; or (d) in order to prevent the commission of a crime by that person.[70] A general comment warranted by this provision is that while it seeks to protect life and implicitly invests in the state the constitutional obligation to prosecute all those responsible for unlawful deprivation of life, it does not outlaw the death penalty. The courts still have the authority to impose the death penalty as the ultimate punishment for the severest crimes such as high treason. While this has the utility of potentially deterring people from committing such crimes,

---

66 Smith Rhona K.M., *Textbook on International Human Rights*, (Oxford University Press, 2007) at pp.194
67 UN Human Rights Committee General Comment 6
68 Smith Rhona, *Textbook on International Human Rights*, supra note 17 at pp.194
69 Article 13(1)
70 Article 13(2)

it remains a question as to how that squares up with the provisions on human dignity and general applicable international human rights law.[71]

Closely connected to the right to life is personal liberty. This is provided for under Article 14(1). Every person shall be entitled to his personal liberty and no person shall be deprived of his personal liberty except in some cases and in accordance with procedure permitted by law. The Article provides these exceptional cases and circumstances as follows: (a) in execution of a sentence or order of a court in respect of a criminal offence of which he has been convicted; or (b) in execution of an order of a court punishing him for contempt of court; or (c) for the purpose of bringing him before a court in execution of an order of a court; or (d) in the case of a person suffering from an infectious or contagious disease, a person of unsound mind, a person addicted to drugs or alcohol or a vagrant, for the purpose of his care or treatment or the protection of the community; or (e) for the purpose of the education or welfare of a person who has not attained the age of eighteen years; or (f) for the purpose of preventing the unlawful entry of that person into Ghana, or of effecting the expulsion, extradition or other lawful removal of that person from Ghana or for the purpose of restricting that person while he is being lawfully conveyed through Ghana in the course of his extradition or removal from one country to another; or (g) upon reasonable suspicion of his having committed or being about to commit a criminal offence under the laws of Ghana.[72] It should be noted that apart from their direct association with the legitimate international concern for the protection of the liberty of persons, these provisions are in direct response to past incidents of arbitrary arrest and detentions in the military regimes of Ghana. However, their value does not only lie in the prohibition of deprivation of liberty, but instead, in the establishment of procedural guarantees and minimum standards for those deprived of their liberty.[73]

Clauses 2 to 7 of Article 14 further amplify the personal liberty right with some procedural rights in criminal cases. These could be said to be personal security rights that help operationalise the right to liberty. They require that a person who is arrested, restricted or detained has the benefit of being

71 The International Covenant on Civil and Political Rights in its Article 6 indicates its abhorrence to the death penalty. Even the Second Optional Protocol to the International Covenant on Civil and Political Rights in its Article 1 requires all State parties to take the necessary measures to abolish the death penalty.
72 Article 14 (1)
73 Smith Rhona Supra note 19 at 226

informed immediately, in a language that he understands, of the reasons for his arrest, restriction or detention and of his right to a lawyer of his choice.[74] Where a person who is arrested, restricted or detained - (a) for the purpose of bringing him before a court in execution of an order of a court; or (b) upon reasonable suspicion of his having committed or being about to commit a criminal offence under the laws of Ghana, and who is not released, shall be brought before a court within forty-eight hours after the arrest, restriction or detention.[75]

If a person arrested, restricted or detained under this article is not tried within a reasonable time, then, without prejudice to any further proceedings that may be brought against him, he shall be released either unconditionally or upon reasonable conditions. This include in particular conditions reasonably necessary to ensure that he appears at a later date for trial or for proceedings preliminary to trial.[76] But where a person is unlawfully arrested, restricted or detained by any other person, s/he shall be entitled to compensation from that other person.[77] Generally, these are checklists against unjustifiable arrests and detentions. They provide criminal suspects of, inter alia, the true benefits of being told of the nature of their crime and a justification for the restriction on their liberty. This has the relevance of cementing the element of predictability in the legal system in relation to criminal justice.

Article 15 provides for Human Dignity as of Right. The dignity of all persons shall be inviolable.[78] Under no circumstance shall a person, whether or not he is arrested, restricted or retained, be subjected to - (a) torture[79] or other cruel, inhuman or degrading treatment or punishment; (b) any other condition that

---

74 Article 14(2)

75 Article 14(3) a&b

76 Article 14(4)

77 Article 14(5)

78 Article 15(1)

79 Though both the courts in Ghana and the Constitution have not defined the term torture, it is expected or likely that the courts would follow the definition given by UN Convention Against Torture and other Cruel, Inhuman or Degrading Treatment or Punishment as "any act by which severe pain or suffering, whether physical or mental, is intentionally inflicted on the person for such purpose as obtaining from him or a third person information or a confession, punishing him for an act he or a third person has committed or is suspected of having committed, or intimidating or coercing him or a third person, or for any reason based on discrimination of any kind, when pain or suffering is inflicted by or at the instigation of or with the consent or acquiescence of a public official or other person acting in an official capacity." (Article 1 United Nations Convention Against Torture 1984)

detracts or is likely to detract from his dignity and worth as a human being.[80] People who have not been convicted of a criminal offence shall not be treated as convicted persons and shall be kept separately from convicted persons.[81] Juvenile offenders who are kept in lawful custody or detention shall be kept separately from adult offenders.[82] It should be observed that Article 16 of the Constitution extends the breadth of Article 15 on the right of the human dignity. It outlaws slavery or servitude.[83] It also frowns upon forced labour except as required by law and endorsed by a court.[84]

Obviously, the overall legal bearing of this provision is the affirmation of the sanctity element of the human person. This is because it is inextricably linked to the humanity of the right-bearer; and the concept of inalienable rights of human beings finds a constitutional anchor in the recognition that it is *not a privilege granted by the state*.[85] Thus acts that seek to undermine or violate the physical and mental integrity such as torture and other degrading treatments of the person are proscribed. Such constitutional jurisprudence reinforces the intrinsic value of the person and affirms the significance of the Kantian injunction to treat every human being as an end and not a means.[86] Understandably, individuals are to be seen and appreciated in their concrete reality, respected for what they represent in a society and not to be merely treated as instruments of the will of others.[87]

Equality rights are contained in Article 17. It provides for equality before the law and outlaws discrimination against all persons on grounds of gender,

---

80 Article 15(2) a & b

81 Article 15(3)

82 82 Article 15(4)

83 Article 16(1)

84 Article 16(2)

85 [Emphasis added] Halton, Cheadle et.al.(ed.), *South Africa Constitutional Law: The Bill of Rights*, (Durban: Butterworths, 2002) at 129.

86 Kommers, *The Constitutional Jurisprudence of the Federal Republic of Germany* 1997 at 313

87 Schackter, "Human Dignity as a Normative Concept" (1983) 77 AJIL 848 cited in Chaskalson, "The Third Bram Fischer Lecture" (2000) 16 South Africa Journal of Human Rights 193 at 198 fn 25

race, colour, ethnic origin, religion, creed or social or economic status.[88] However, the provision prima facie permits Parliament to enact laws aimed among others, at redressing social, economic or educational imbalance in the Ghanaian society.[89] It is noted that the concept of equality is rooted in philosophical debates[90], a detailed analysis of which is out with the scope of this paper. However, the human rights jurisprudence of democratic states has long concerned itself with inequalities. Not only is the equality as of right accepted as a cornerstone of democratic states but also the prohibition of discrimination is premised on the assertion that all people are born free and equal in dignity and rights.[91] This demands the recognition of all persons as having equal rights with the aim of according them equal opportunities for free and full development.[92] Thus constitutional rights on the elimination of discrimination do not seek to treat people as if they were equal but to redress factual inequalities in the enjoyment of human rights.[93] Equality before the law gives to all persons in Ghana equal access to the courts and to be viewed in law in a non-discriminatory manner, especially with respect to the

---

88 Article 17(1) &(2). But note that Clause 3 of article 17 expands the list of grounds of discrimination. It states as follows: For the purposes of this article, "discriminate" means to give different treatment to different persons attributable only or mainly to their respective descriptions by race, place of origin, political opinions, colour, gender, occupation, religion or creed, whereby persons of one description are subjected to disabilities or restrictions to which persons of another description are not made subject or are granted privileges or advantages which are not granted to persons of another description. This perhaps is comparable to some international humans rights instruments such as: International Covenant on Civil and Political Rights (1976)(ICCPR), [race, colour, sex, language, religion, political or other opinion, national or social origin, property, birth or other status, Article 2(1)]; International Covenant on Economic, Social and Cultural Rights (1976) (ICESCR), [race, colour, sex, language, religion, political or other opinion, national or social origin, property, birth or other status, Article 2(2)]; Universal Declaration of Human Rights (1948) (UNDHR),[ race, colour, sex, language, religion, political or other opinion, national or social origin, property, birth or other status, Article 2) and Article of Africa Charter on Human and Peoples Rights.
89 Article 17(4)
90 Smith Rhona at pp.191
91 Article 1 of UNDHR
92 Smith Rhona, at pp.192
93 Ibid

judicial determination of their rights and freedoms under the Constitution, 1992.[94] Nevertheless, the central force of this right is dependent upon the existence of other rights. That is, it could be a sheer empty political gesture to constitutionalise this right if other rights are denied. One can only claim the right not to be discriminated against only if one has a right to what is claimed.[95]

The most comprehensive provision for due process rights in criminal justice and civil trials or proceedings are contained in Article 19. Perhaps it codifies the natural justice rules of fair trial. For instance, a criminal suspect must be given a fair hearing within a reasonable time by a court.[96] In addition, any person charged with a criminal offence shall be presumed to be innocent until he is proved or has pleaded guilty[97] and be informed immediately in a language that he understands, and in detail; of the nature of the offence charged.[98] In the words of the Article in question, such a person would be deemed to have been given a fair hearing and trial if given adequate time and facilities for the preparation of his or her defence[99] and permitted to defend himself or herself before the court in person or by a lawyer of his choice.[100] An Accused person is to be afforded facilities to examine, in person or by his lawyer, the witnesses called by the prosecution before the court, and to obtain the attendance and carry out the examination of witnesses to testify on the same conditions as those applicable to witnesses called by the prosecution.[101] In repudiating retroactive criminal punishment, Article 19 further provides that no person shall be charged with or held to be guilty of a criminal offence which is founded on an act or omission that did not at the time it took place constitute an offence.[102]

---

94 See Stavros, S., *The Guarantees for the Accused Person Under Article 6 of the European Convention on Human Rights – An Analysis of the Application of the Convention and a Comparison with other Instruments*, (The Hague: Kluwer, 1993) and Weissbrodt, D., *The Right to a Fair Trial under the Universal Declaration of Human Rights and the International Covenant on Civil and Political Rights – Background, Development and Interpretation*, ( The Hague: Kluwer, 2001)
95 Stanley Corbett, *Canadian Human Rights Law and Commentary*, (LexisNexis Canada Inc. 2007) at pp.25
96 Article 19(1)
97 Article 19(1)c
98 Article 19(1)d
99 Article 19(1)e
100 Article 19(1)f
101 Article 19(1)g
102 Article 19(5)

It is the opinion of this writer that this provision necessitates three short comments. First of all, one of the cornerstones of the rule of law itself is the notion of a fair trial. This requires certainty and predictability of legal rules. In that case, the constitutional prohibition on retroactive penal legislation seeks to give meaning to the legal principle that a person cannot be punished for something which was not a crime at the time it was committed – *nullum crimen sine lege and nulla poena sine lege*. Besides, adequate time and facilities accorded to an accused person fosters fairness in the trial process and prevents trial by surprise. Lastly, the presumption of innocence of an accused is an open but fair invitation to the courts to commence the trial proceedings with an open mind and no preconceived notion of guilt. This makes the right of a defence constitutionally meaningful.

Articles 23 and 296 further ground the codification of natural justice principles in the Constitution. These provisions extend the scope and applicability of the natural justice rules of fair trial in criminal justice to administrative matters. Indeed, their primary end is administrative justice. Administrative bodies and administrative officials are obliged to act fairly and reasonably; and to comply with the requirements imposed on them by law; and persons aggrieved by the exercise of such acts and decisions shall have the right to seek redress before a court or other tribunal.[103] Where discretionary power is vested in any person or authority, it is deemed to imply a duty to be fair and candid and the exercise of the discretionary power shall not be arbitrary, capricious or biased either by resentment, prejudice or personal dislike and shall be in accordance with due process of law.[104]

These Articles are not bereft of constitutional relevance, particularly to the human rights project in Ghana. Clearly, on the one hand, they seek to respect the constitutional doctrine of separation of powers by allowing administrators the latitude to perform their legitimate functions. On the other hand, they throw in a caution that the administrative discretion is not absolute so as to allow corrupt and despotic administrators to wreak injustice.[105] The requirement of reasonability or rationality in the merit or outcome of the administrative decision must be met. Therefore, it can be argued that the Constitution seeks to give full expression to its fundamental values of accountability, probity, justice and openness.[106]

103 Article 23
104 Article 296 (a) & (b)
105 Halton, Cheadle et.al.(ed.), *South Africa Constitutional Law: The Bill of Rights*, at pp.611-12
106 Preamble, The Constitution of the Republic of Ghana, 1992.

Article 21 of the Constitution contains the general fundamental freedoms. These include freedoms of speech, expression, press and media, thought, conscience and belief, academic freedom, religion, assembly, association, information and movement.[107] Meanwhile, these freedoms are supported by property and privacy rights lumped together in Article 18 of the Constitution. However, limitations on these freedoms are permitted on such grounds as are reasonably required in the interest of defence, public safety, public health or the running of essential services and laws as are necessary in a democratic society.[108] While these freedoms elicit various comments from human rights scholars, one may note here that the inclusion of the "running of essential services" in the limitation clause on these freedoms is worrisome. It is unclear what a politically zealous judiciary would do with it in the enforcement of constitutional rights. In my opinion, such a provision is a source for gratuitous judicial speculation on the nature and scope of limitation of fundamental freedoms guaranteed in democratic regimes. Perhaps this may not be an enduring evaluation if the courts in Ghana develop on the facts of a given case, a reasonable test to control or clearly define the ambit of such a limiting element in the provision.

Finally, democratic participatory rights to citizens are guaranteed under Article 42 of the Constitution. It entitles citizens who are eighteen years of age or above, and of sound mind, the right to vote in all public elections and referenda.[109] Perhaps this reinforces Article 1 of the Constitution which vests the sovereignty of Ghana in the people. This major right though limited, allows the people to exercise this sovereign power by participating in crucial public decisions that go to the future, and governance of the nation. It is a clear rejection of rule by the gun and an affirmation of the commitment of the people to a civil process of governance in the hope of reaping the blessings of liberty, justice and prosperity.

### Economic, Social and Cultural Rights

For the first time in the constitutional history of Ghana, the Constitution, 1992 has provided for Socio-Economic rights, though they are not as detailed as expected. Those limited provisions on the subject matter of socio-economic

107 Article 21(1) a, b, c, d, e, f, &g
108 Article 21(4)
109 Article 42

rights in the Constitution appear to be a replica of those in the International Covenant on Social, Economic and Cultural Rights. A number of reasoned justifications could be advanced for their inclusion in the Constitution. In part, the framers have shown a concern to identify the provisions of the Constitution with the prevailing international human rights regime. Besides, taking these rights seriously implies a commitment to social integration, solidarity and equality, including tackling the question of income distribution[110] in the larger Ghanaian society. Economic, Social and Cultural rights ineluctably illustrate a major concern for the protection of vulnerable groups, such as the poor and the handicapped.[111] Fundamental needs as these rights seek to provide and protect, should not be at the mercy of changing governmental policies and programmes, but should be defined as entitlements.[112]

An explicit human right to receive education with a corresponding duty of the state to provide for this education is guaranteed under Article 25 of the Constitution, 1992. All persons shall have the right to equal educational opportunities and facilities.[113] For the full realisation of this right, basic education shall be free, compulsory and available to all.[114] Of particular importance is the fact that the obligation on the state to ensure a basic education is not qualified by reference to progressive realisation or resource constraints. In addition, it does preclude a system which permits the charging of school fees at the basic level. Conversely, secondary education in its different forms, including technical and vocational education, shall be made generally available and accessible to all by every appropriate means, and in particular, by the progressive introduction of free education.[115]

It is further provided that higher education like university education shall be made equally accessible to all, on the basis of capacity, by every appropriate means.[116] Also, the state is constitutionally bound to respect individual rights to establish at their own expense private schools subject to the laws of the state.[117] Moreover, given the higher level of illiteracy rate in

110 Asbjorn Eide et al ed., *Economic, Social and Cultural Rights*, (Martinus Nijhoff Publishers, 2001)
111 ibid at pp.5
112 Ibid at 6
113 Article 25(1)
114 Article 25(1)a
115 Article 25(1)b
116 Article 25(1)c
117 Article 25(2)

the country, particularly in the rural communities, the provision in question attempts a solution by providing that functional literacy shall be encouraged or intensified as far as possible. It could be said that the provision for the right to education is in accord with the growing international consensus that education is imperative to enable the individual to freely develop his or her talent, personality and dignity, to actively participate in a free society and to contribute to the tolerance and respect for human rights.[118]

Article 24 provides for the rights to work under satisfactory, safe and healthy conditions[119] save that this is not a right entitling people to a job. However, workers are also entitled to equal pay for equal work without distinction of any kind.[120] Additionally, every worker is entitled to rest, leisure and reasonable limitation of working hours and periods of holidays with pay, as well as remuneration for public holidays.[121] People within working environments are entitled to form or join a trade union of their choice for the promotion and protection of their economic and social interests.[122] However, such rights could be restricted by law and on grounds as are reasonably necessary in the interest of national security or public order or for the protection of the rights and freedoms of others.[123] Regardless of these limitations, the provision symbolises a constitutional jurisprudence that stresses interdependence between labour conditions and social justice. It enhances the concept of labour as a human value, social need and a means for the self-realisation and development of human personality. But recourse must be had to the revealing insufficiency character of this Article. Indeed, it does not in any way entitle any one a right to be provided with work by the state. It merely provides for rights in work.

Cultural rights are explicitly guaranteed under Article 26. Under this article every person is entitled to enjoy, practise, profess, maintain and promote any culture, language, tradition or religion subject to the provisions of this Constitution.[124] Perhaps a persuasive reason for such a provision is the need to respect the cultural values of groups and individuals by others who may not share these values. But the provision excluded from its ambit and protection

118 See Mialaret, G., "What Kind of Education?", in G. Mialaret (ed.), The Child's Right to Education, 1979, at pp.47-53.
119 Article 24(1)
120 ibid
121 Article 24(2)
122 Article 24(3)
123 Article 24(4)
124 Article 26(1)

all customary practices which dehumanise or are injurious to the physical and mental well-being of a person.[125] Within the cultural context of Ghana, it is fair to say that this provision has in its contemplation obsolete cultural practices like widowhood rites, trial by ordeal, female genital mutilation, witches camps, and host of others. These practices are dehumanising and they affect the mental and physical wellbeing of the victims. Thus the provision seeks to cure the defects of such cultural practices by excluding them from constitutional protection as they fell below the benchmark of human dignity.

### Women and Children's Rights

One key feature that distinguishes the *Fourth Republican Constitution*, 1992 from the Second and Third Republican Constitutions of 1969 and 1979 respectively, is the provisions on women and children's rights. Article 27(1) provides that special care shall be accorded to mothers during a reasonable period before and after child-birth and during those periods, working mothers shall be accorded paid leave. Also, facilities shall be provided for the care of children below school-going age to enable women, who have the traditional care for children, realise their full potential.[126] The provision ends with an explicit guarantee for equal training and promotion rights to women without any impediments from any person.[127] Women's rights as captured here, in part, represent a legitimate force in the Ghanaian society to address serious gender related issues brought about by a long period of negative social construction. An arbitrary societal consignment of women to the roles of housekeeping, child care or babysitting weakens women's ability to work during such periods as before and after child-birth. By implication, their economic and social vulnerability in society is exacerbated. At best, it cripples any progressive move by women to realise their potentials during such periods. It is argued here that Article 27 of the Constitution, in theory, drowns this culturally imposed inequity in the larger Ghanaian society and generates an optimistic feeling in the people that culturally contemptuous treatment of women is over.

Under Article 28(1) Parliament has a mandatory constitutional duty to enact such laws as are necessary to ensure the realisation of the rights of children. This provision defines a child as a person below eighteen years of

125 Article 26(2)
126 Article 27(2)
127 Article 27(3)

age.[128] Children are entitled under the Constitution to special care, assistance and maintenance as is necessary for their development from their natural parents.[129] This right can only be limited in circumstances where parents have effectively surrendered their rights and responsibilities in respect of a child in accordance with law.[130] Moreover, children are entitled to a reasonable provision out of the estate of their parents whether or not born in wedlock.[131] The interest of the child shall be paramount in all activities relating to its maintenance and upbringing.[132] In that case, children and young persons shall receive special protection against exposure to physical and moral hazards[133] and be protected from engaging in work that constitutes a threat to their health, education or development.[134]

The Constitution prohibits all acts that subject children to torture or other cruel, inhuman or degrading treatment or punishment.[135] Above all, no child shall be deprived by any other person of medical treatment, education or any other social or economic benefit by reason only of religious or other beliefs.[136] Apart from the fact that this appears to be an incorporation of some provisions of the Convention on the Right of the Child (CRC), it has a peculiar Constitutional relevance to Ghana with regard to the pervasive problems of child labour and child neglect. Children need protection from callous parents and general societal neglect. This provision signifies hope for children who are often denied the benefits of care by outdated customs. It also saves children from the possible engagement in hazardous works that turns to be injurious to their health or mental and physical wellbeing.

### Rights of Disabled and Sick Persons

Like the women and children's rights identified in the preceding pages, the rights of the disabled and sick persons are a peculiar feature of the Fourth Republican Constitution, 1992. Perhaps they came as a direct response to

128 Article 28(5)
129 Article 28(1)a
130 Ibid
131 Article 28(1)b
132 Article 28(1)c
133 Article 28(1)d
134 Article 28(2)
135 Article 28 (3)
136 Article 28(4)

increased national and international concerns for the protection of the disabled and the sick in society. Article 29(1) accorded disabled persons the right to live with their families or with foster parents and to participate in social, creative or recreational activities. They are not to be subjected to differential treatment in respect of their residence other than that required by their condition or by the improvement which they may derive from the treatment.[137] Additionally, disabled persons shall be protected against all exploitation, regulations and treatment of a discriminatory, abusive or degrading nature.[138] In fact, in any judicial proceedings in which a disabled person is a party, the legal procedure applied shall take his or her physical and mental condition into account.[139] Likewise, as far as practicable, every place with public access should have appropriate facilities for disabled persons.[140] In terms of their direct participation in the economic sphere of the country, disabled persons who are engaged in business or employed in business organisations are entitled to special incentives.[141] However, Parliament has the institutional burden to enact the laws necessary to ensure the enforcement of these provisions.[142]

Article 30 contains the special rights of the sick. It provides that a person who by reason of sickness or any other cause is unable to give his consent shall not be deprived by any other person of medical treatment, education or any other social or economic benefit by reason only of religious or other beliefs.[143] This will potentially save the sick from certain religious practices which tend to deny the sick certain medical benefits. However, the rights discussed in this paper are not exhaustive. Article 33(5) states: "The rights, duties, declarations and guarantees relating to the fundamental human rights and freedoms specifically mentioned in this Chapter shall not be regarded as excluding others not specifically mentioned, which are considered to be inherent in a democracy and intended to secure the freedom and dignity of man." More extensive provisions with related socio-economic rights values are listed under Chapter 6. These are known as the Directive Principles of State Policy, and have been held by Ghana's Supreme Court[144] to be justiciable

137 Article 29(2)
138 Article (4)
139 Article 29(5)
140 Article 29(6)
141 Article 29(7)
142 Article 29(8).
143 Article 30
144 See the 31st. December Case, The CIBA Case and Ghana's Lottery's Case

under the appropriate circumstances. There is a presumption in favour of the justiciability of all the socio-economic rights contained under chapter 6. Accordingly, potential rights claimants can still rely on these provisions for the enforcement of such rights as inherent in a democracy and which intends to secure the freedom and dignity of man.

## Conclusion

But what does all this mean to the human rights student or practitioner in Ghana? First, it shows that the human rights structure sits in well with the International Bill of Rights, a position within the context of the evolutionary theory, and does not clearly deny universality of human rights. But it does not also reject the Afrocentric claims as there are not only cultural rights which must be given local content, but may balance values of individuality and community in their application. That is, while the content and validity of such rights might be based on the mores of a particular community, the test of limitation on such rights might not necessarily be based on the exclusive values of that community. For instance, the dehumanisation and mental and physical wellbeing requirements in Article 26 are capable of a wider construction with reference to values that may have minimum universal moral values.

Nevertheless the justificatory theory may have a problem; it is not completely out of place as the limitation clauses on the enforcement of rights includes issues like, public order, the running of essential services, public health, and national security. Contemporary human rights theory does accept these as a reasonable basis for limiting human rights. However, an interpretation of these concepts may not be accepted if such an interpretation is based on a dubious understanding of a necessity of national unity and political stability. Besides, culture may have a value and people can explore their unique cultural values to develop themselves, but culture cannot exclusively be relied upon to justify violation of human rights. The uniqueness of culture must be accepted in any human rights discourse, but the value of culture must justifiably be mediated by other fundamental values of a legal system which form the bases of other rights and freedoms.

Finally, the protection and enforcement camp, as shown from the bare description and limited commentary of the 1992 Constitution above, gestures to a robust constitutional protection of human rights. But as we have shown above mere provisions of human rights in a constitution will not suffice. The courts through the assistance of the BAR and civil society will aid with the realisation of those rights. Thus, for the human rights structure of Ghana to be strong and useful for the legal system, we need an independent judiciary with sufficient knowledge of the law, strong BAR, strong civil society and a strong Constitution – sufficient provisions protecting human rights and freedoms. All of these should be supported by the appropriate political culture supporting a human rights culture.

## 3
# ADJUDICATION OF HUMAN RIGHTS CASES BY THE COURTS

## Mavis Ekua Enyamah Kwainoe

**Abstract**

It is truism that democracy is threatened in the absence of respect and recognition for human rights. The 1992 Constitution of Ghana provide for civil and political rights, socio-cultural rights and economic rights. All persons, whether natural or juristic are under a constitutional mandate to respect and uphold the fundamental human rights recognized under Ghana's Constitutional dispensation. The paper interrogates the jurisprudence of the Ghanaian Courts in the enforcement and adjudication of human rights disputes. The paper considers issues of locus standi, the reliefs obtainable and developing issues concerning the enforcement and adjudication of human rights disputes. This paper acknowledges that the naturalist's perspective of human rights is very operational in Ghana and that the courts will at all times seek the enforcement of any right that satisfies the tests of being inherent in a democracy and intended to secure the freedom and dignity of man.

**Introduction**

It is an truism that democracy is threatened in the absence of respect and recognition for human rights. Increasingly, the recognition of human rights among the comity of nations has advanced from the known traditional rights as the right to life and freedom of speech to such rights as the right to be forgotten as recognized among nations like the United States of America.

The 1992 Constitution of Ghana proclaims these rights under Chapters 5[1] and 6.[2] These chapters provide for civil and political rights, socio-cultural rights and economic rights. All persons, whether natural or juristic are under a constitutional mandate to respect and uphold the fundamental human rights recognized under Ghana's Constitutional dispensation. These rights are enjoyed by both citizens and non-citizens and cannot be derogated from unless sanctioned by law.[3]

The present topic invites an interrogation of the jurisprudence of the Ghanaian Courts in the enforcement and adjudication of human rights disputes. The paper shall be structured in four parts. The first part shall attempt a definition of human rights. This part shall also consider some of the human rights guaranteed under the Constitution and the attitude of the courts in their enforcement and recognition. Part two shall consider the enforcement of fundamental human rights in Ghana. This part will entail a discussion of the jurisdiction of the courts, issues of locus standi and the reliefs obtainable. Part three focuses on developing issues concerning the enforcement and adjudication of human rights disputes. The final part shall be the conclusion and reflections.

## Human Rights Defined

Despite the various strands of definition of human rights in the literature, the consensus appears to be of two schools of thought. The first, the broader view is grounded in natural law and the other, the restricted view  on the positivist school of thought. The naturalists view human rights as entitlements or claims  that human beings are entitled by virtue of  their humanity.[4] This thinking views human rights as an inherent entitlement of man. Therefore, in so far as a person is a human being, he ought to be accorded and enjoy such rights. For the positivists, human rights are nothing but entitlements proclaimed by the law to be enjoyed by human beings. Therefore, the test

1 Chapter 5 of the Constitution constitutionalises the fundamental human rights
2 This chapter contains the directive principles of state policy.
3 Article 12 of the 1992 Constitution.
4 Jack Donnelly, 'Universal Human Rights: In Theory and Practice' (2003) Cornel University Press,1-19.

for the enjoyment here must be based on it being posited in a written law. The positivists school will therefore, not recognize any right as a human right unless the law sanctions same.

Depending on its nature and character, a particular right may be classified as fundamental. Fundamental human rights however, differ from jurisdictions. In Ghana, chapter 5 of the Constitution, 1992 recognizes some of these fundamental human rights as the right to life, freedom of speech, freedom of movement, privacy rights, fair trial rights and spousal rights.

The essence for the respect for fundamental human rights has been captured under the first international instrument on human rights, the 1948 Universal Declaration of Human Rights. The declaration proclaims that recognition of these rights is the foundation of "freedom, justice and peace in the world."[5] These rights, at the very least defines the essence of man. It seeks to uphold the dignity of human beings, ensures and promotes justice, equity and equality. Their recognition and enforcement promotes accountability of institutions and upholds the democratic credentials of the state.

## Fundamental Human Rights under the 1992 Constitution of Ghana

Two chapters of the Constitution have been devoted to human rights. Chapters 5 and 6 focus on fundamental human rights and directive principles of state policy. The rights as recognized under chapter 6 of the Constitution are mainly economic the character and are only presumed justiciable.[6] Article 12 of the 1992 Constitution under Chapter 5 of the Constitution proclaims that:

*(1) The fundamental human rights and freedom enshrined in the chapter shall be respected and upheld by the Executive, Legislature and Judiciary and all other organs of government and its agencies and, where applicable to them, by all natural and legal persons in Ghana, and shall be enforce by the Courts as provided for in this Constitution.*

As provided in clause 2 of Article 12, the fundamental human rights as recognized under the Constitution must be respected by all persons, whether natural or artificial and whether as citizens or not.

---

5 Preamble to the Universal Declaration of Human Rights.
6 *Ghana Lotto Operators Association and Others v National Lottery Authority* [2007-2008] 2 SCGLR 1088.

The Constitution 1992, seems to have been grounded on the naturalist perspective of human rights as the rights are not limited to only those that are expressly provided for in the Constitution. Article 33(5) of the Constitution states that:

> *The rights, duties, declarations and guarantees relating to the fundamental human rights and freedoms specifically mentioned in this Chapter shall not be regarded as excluding others not specifically mentioned which are considered to be inherent in a democracy and intended to secure the freedom and dignity of man.*

Thus, where a person can demonstrate that a particular right is inherent in a democracy and that that right is intended to secure his freedom and dignity as man, he shall be entitled to the enjoyment of such right although the right may not have been expressly provided for in the 1992 Constitution of Ghana. The enjoyment of rights in Ghana is however, not absolute. It is subject to the larger public interest and the respect of the rights of others.[7] It needs further mention that the enjoyment of rights is associated with the correlated obligation of the performance of duties.[8]

## Selected Rights under the 1992 Constitution of Ghana
### *Civil, political and socio –economic rights*

The 1992 Constitution provides for several rights that may be categorized into civil and political rights, socio-cultural rights and economic rights. The Constitution makes provision for the protection of life, protection of personal liberty, respect for human dignity, protection form slavery, protection of privacy of home and other property, fair trial, equality and freedom from discrimination, property rights of spouses, administrative justice, educational rights, cultural rights and practices, women's rights, children's rights, rights of disabled person, rights of the sick and protection of rights by the courts.

---

7 Article 12(2).

8 Article 41 obliges citizens to inter alia promote the prestige and good name of Ghana, uphold and respect the laws of Ghana, respect the rights and freedoms of others and generally contribute to the development and well-being of the State.

## Civil and Political Rights: Freedom of speech and expression

The freedom of all persons in Ghana to speech and expression is guaranteed under Article 21(1)(a) of the Constitution, 1992. This freedom has been augmented by press freedom and freedom of the individual as guaranteed under Article 162(1)-(4). This freedom is held in high esteem in every liberal democracy. It is an avenue for citizens and other stakeholders to put the ruling government on its toes through constructive criticisms. As noted by Article 12(2) of the Constitution, the enjoyment of rights must be correlated with the respect of the rights of others. Failure of a person to exercise his or her right to free speech and press in tune with the constitutional sanctions may lead to the tortious action of defamation or even contempt.

In the Supreme Court case of *New Patriotic Party v Ghana Broadcasting Corporation,*[9] the Supreme Court had the occasion to pronounce on the freedom of expression and speech under the Constitution, 1992. The facts of the case are that in 1993, when the Budget Statement of the Government of Ghana was read, it sparked several controversies and criticisms among the general public. As a result, the Minister of Finance on behalf of the government appeared on radio and television to defend the budget. The plaintiff, a registered political party and then the main opposition party applied to the defendant, a statutory body responsible for radio and television broadcasting to be allowed air time to also present its views on the budget. This application was however refused by the defendant. The Plaintiff sued in the Supreme Court for a declaration that the defendant's conduct was a violation of its rights under Articles 55(11) and 163 of the 1992 Constitution. More so, it argued that the defendant breached its right to freely express itself when it refused to grant it airtime.

The Supreme Court unanimously held that the defendant's refusal to allow the Plaintiff airtime amounted to institutional pre-selection of information to the public which was against the spirit of the Constitution. The Court emphasized that the said refusal was an unnecessary fetter on the plaintiff's freedom of expression and the right to information of the Ghanaian populace. At page 373 Justice Amua-Sekyi intoned persuasively as follows *"The temptation to ride roughshod over the opinions of others must be resisted; for it is only through the free flow of ideas and discussion that error is exposed, truth vindicated and liberty preserved."*

9 [1993-94] 2 GLR 354

However, in the case of **Republic v Independent Media Corporation of Ghana (Radio Eye Case)**[10] the Supreme Court reiterated that the enjoyment of this right is not absolute. As justice Acquah noted in that case, there is the need for "some form of regulatory measures and limitations" as they are "essential to ensure sane and healthy establishment and operation of broadcasting services."[11] These two cases supra clearly show the ambit of the right to free speech in Ghana. Whiles *NPP v GBC* received recognition and enforcement, the Radio Eye Case cautioned against abuse of this right. Members of the public must therefore be measured in their utterances so as not to be caught in abusing the enjoyment of this right.

## Freedom of Association and the Courts

On the freedom of association, one scholar, Alexis de Tocqueville has posited as follows:

> *The most natural privilege of man, next to the right of acting for himself, is that of combining his exertions with those of his fellow creatures and of acting in common with them. The right of association therefore appears to me almost as inalienable in its nature as the right of personal liberty. No legislator can attack it without impairing the foundations of society.*

This reflection is constitutionalised under Article 21(1)(e) of the 1992 Constitution. The Article provides for the freedom of association of all persons including the right to form and or join trade unions or other associations be they national or international. In realizing this right, the state has been duty bound under Article 37(2) to put in mechanisms.

The case of **Mensima & Others v Attorney-General**[12] presented the Supreme Court of Ghana with the opportunity to uphold this right. The plaintiff submitted before the Supreme Court that the Manufacture and Sale of Spirits Regulation 1962 (LI 239) an existing law, which required the plaintiffs as a pre-condition to distilling akpeteshie to belong to a registered distillers co-operative society. More so, the joining of such corporation was essential to the granting of a licence to the plaintiff to operate their distillery. The Supreme

10 [1996-97] SCGLR 258
11 p283.
12 (1996-97) SCGLR 676

Court however declared the said law unconstitutional as violating the freedom of association of the plaintiffs. Justice Acquah asserted that *"the essence of freedom of association is the liberty or lack of compulsion on the individual to form or join an association."*[13] He noted that the right of association includes the right not to associate with persons one does not wish to associate with.

The above authority teaches the lesson that, no person can be forced to exercise his right or freedom guaranteed under the Constitution and that any attempt to fetter same will receive resistance from the courts.

In *New Patriotic Party v Attorney –General (CIBA Case)*[14] the Supreme Court again upheld the freedom of association guaranteed under the Constitution, 1992. In this case, the plaintiff challenged the constitutionality of the *Council of Indigenous Business Association Law, 1993 (PNDCL 312)*. The law required certain associations specified in its schedule to be compulsorily registered with the Council. More so, the Council was to be controlled by a Minister of State. The court was thus called upon to answer the question whether the compulsory registration with the Council and ministerial control was a violation of the Association's right to form or join an association of their choice. The Supreme Court answered this in the affirmative. Bamford Addo JSC (as she then was) pronounced as follows *"Freedom of association means freedom of the people to voluntarily join together to form associations for the protection of their interests free from state interference. This freedom is effectively taken away in this case by the compulsion of the stated organisations to join CIBA..."*[15]

## The Courts and Freedom of Assembly and the Right to Demonstrate

The freedom to freely assemble and demonstrate, seen as a fundamental freedom is considered a pillar in ensuring healthy multi-party democracy. Article 21(1)(d) of the 1992 Constitution allows for the free exercise of the right to assemble and take part in demonstrations and processions subject to the public interest. The attitude of the courts in Ghana with regards to this freedom was demonstrated in the case of *New Patriotic Party v Inspector General of Police*[16]. The Plaintiffs in this case , then the main opposition party

13 at 715.
14 [1996-97] SCGLR 929.
15 at 751.
16 [1993-94]2 GLR 459.

staged a demonstration in Accra against the government's budget. The police however stormed the demonstration and dispersed the crowd on the grounds that the Plaintiff failed to obtain a permit as required by the then *Public Order Decree, 1972 (NRCD 68)*. The Plaintiff therefore, brought an action challenging the constitutionality of sections 7,8, 12(c) and 13 of NRCD 68 on the grounds that those sections violated the right to demonstrate guaranteed under Article 21(1)(d) of the Constitution upon the requirement of a permit.

In a unanimous decision, the Supreme Court held that sections 7,8 and 13 of NRCD 68 violated the right of assembly on the account of their requirement for a prior permit. For Justice Hayfron-Benjamin, the Constitution 1992 was *"intended that the citizens of this country should enjoy the fullest measure of responsible Human and Civil Rights. Therefore, any law which seeks to abridge these Rights and Freedoms must be struck down as unconstitutional. The requirement of a permit or licence is one of such abridgement of the constitutional right."*[17]

## Rights of Disabled Persons

Article 29 of the 1992 Constitution proclaims the rights of disabled persons in Ghana. Under the said provision, disabled persons have the right to live with their families or with foster parents and also to participate in social, creative or recreational activities.[18] A person who is disabled must not be subjected to differential treatment in respect of his residence other than that required by his condition or by the improvement which he may derive from the treatment.[19] Further if the stay of a disabled person in a specialized establishment is indispensable, the environment and living conditions there shall be as close as possible to those of the normal life of a person of his age. In administering justice, the courts are under a constitutional duty to take into account the physical and mental conditions of any person who is disabled and who is a party to the action.[20] The Constitution further requires that public places provide appropriate facilities for disabled persons and finally, the Constitution under Article 29(7) requires that special incentive be given to disabled persons engaged in business and also to business organisations that employ disabled persons in significant numbers.

In conformity with Articles 29(8) and 37(2)(b), Parliament has enacted

17 Ibid, 505-506.
18 Article 29(1) of the 1992 Constitution.
19 Article 29(2).
20 Article 29(5).

the Persons with Disability Act, 2006 (Act 715) to detail out and fortify the rights of disabled persons guaranteed under the 1992 Constitution. Whereas the courts will uphold the existence of these rights of the disabled, some of their enforcement being positive in character may pose certain challenges. This is mainly due to them being contingent on the availability of resources. Therefore, the absence of such resources could lead to their denial.[21] It is however hoped that our courts will continue to influence political decisions in order to fully ensure the enjoyment of this right as happens in jurisdictions such as South Africa, Norway and Philippines.[22]

### Administrative Justice as a Fundamental Human Right

The 1992 Constitution under Articles 19, 23 and 296 provides for the rules of natural justice in relation to the performance of the functions of administrative bodies, officials and persons exercising discretionary power. In particular, Article 19 incorporates rules on fair trials in criminal matters. Even in civil actions, Article 19 (13) of the Constitution, 1992 demands that their adjudication be fair. Article 23 requires administrative tribunals and officials to comply with the due process of law. Likewise the requirement that due process be followed in the exercise of discretionary powers by state officials have been provided for under Article 296 of the 1992 Constitution.

On the requirement that administrative bodies and persons exercising discretionary powers follow due process and also comply with the rules of natural justice, the case of *Awuni v West African Examination Council*[23] is apposite. In this case, following a preliminary investigation that established that the plaintiff had engaged in examination malpractices, the defendant cancelled the result of the appellant and twelve others. According to the defendant, the cancellation decision undertaken was necessary to protect the sanctity of the examination. Further, according to them, the examination malpractices were apparent and hence there was no need for the Appellant to be invited. However, the court held that by not inviting the appellant before cancelling the result, the defendant had breached the *audi alteram partem* rule

---

21 This is reflected in Article 38(3) of the Constitution 1992 which provides inter alia that ' the state shall subject to the availability of resources provide ...resettlement of disabled persons.'
22 See for instance the South African case of *Minister of Health and Others v Treatment Campaign and Others* [No. 2] CCT8//02A the South African Supreme court held that it could make orders impacting on the policy of the government provided that the laws or the Constitution envisaged a basic item for the citizenry.
23 [2003-2004] SCGLR 471.

of natural justice and that was a violation of Article 23 of the Constitution. The court noted that the conduct of the defendant was not fair and same was unreasonable. Sophia Akuffo JSC (as she then was) stated that *"Where a body or officer has an administrative function to perform, the activity must be conducted with, and reflect qualities of fairness, reasonableness and legal compliance."*[24]

In a similar tone, Kpegah JSC (As he then was) pronounced as follows:

> I cannot contemplate how a person could be said to have acted fairly and reasonably if he did not give either notice or hearing to another who was entitled to such notice or hearing before taking a decision which adversely affects his rights..."[25]

The constitutional demand that administrative bodies, institutions and persons exercising discretionary powers follow due process of law in the execution of their mandate is very crucial in ensuring that the fundamental human rights guaranteed under the constitution is not infringed upon by these bodies and or persons under the altar of administrative function.

## The Ghanaian Courts and Socio-Economic Rights

Socio-economic rights under the 1992 Constitution include the right to education, property rights, rights of workers in employment and property rights of spouses. Such other socio-economic rights as the right to water, food, adequate housing and health care have not had express provision in the Constitution. However as provided for under Article 33(5) of the Constitution 1992, these rights are enforceable if an applicant can satisfy the court that they are inherent in a democracy and intended to secure the freedom and dignity of man.

The realization of most of these socio-economic rights have been provided for under Chapter 6 of the Constitution which contains the Directive Principles of State Policy.[26]

24 At page 514

25 At page 489

26 Per Article 34(1) of the Constitution, 1992, the Directive Principles of State Policy shall guide 'all citizens, Parliament, the President, the Judiciary, the Council of State, the Cabinet, political parties and other bodies and persons in applying or interpreting the Constitution or any other law and in making and implementing any policy decisions, for the establishment of a just and free society.'

The debate on the justiciability or otherwise of the directive principles of state policy is now settled in the case of ***Ghana Lotto Operators Association and others v National Lottery Authority*** [2007-2008] 2 SCGLR 1088. The Supreme Court speaking through Date-Bah JSC (as he then was) held that:

> A presumption of jusiciablity in respect of Chapter 6 of the Constitution would strengthen the legal status of ESC human rights in the Ghanaian jurisdiction. Of course, there may be particular provisions in Chapter 6 which do not lend themselves to enforcement by a court. The very nature of such a particular provision would rebut the presumption of justiciablity in relation to it. In the absence of a demonstration that a particular provision does not lend itself to enforcement by courts, the enforcement by this Court of the obligations imposed in Chapter 6 should be insisted upon and would be a way of deepening our democracy and the liberty under the law it entails. Applying this presumption of justiciability, our view is that the economic objectives laid out in Article 36 of the Constitution are legally binding and are not merely a matter of conscience for successive government of our land. The objectives, have though, to be liberally construed in order not to interfere with the democratic mandates of successive governments.

Per this decision therefore, the directive principles of state policy, which mainly centers on the realization of the economic rights of the state must be presumed justiciable unless the very nature of that right does not lend itself to being justiciable. For instance, the courts are likely to hold as not justiciable such rights which are positive in character and a *sine qua non* to their enjoyment is the availability of resources.[27]

### The Jurisdiction in Human Rights Cases in Ghana

Under the 1992 Constitution, it is only the High Court that has exclusive original jurisdiction in the enforcement of fundamental human rights. This jurisdiction of the High Court is noted in Article 140(2) of the Constitution which provides that "The High Court shall have jurisdiction to enforce the

---

27 *Federation of Youth Associations of Ghana (FEDYAG) (No 2) v Public Universities of Ghana& Ors* [2011] 2 SCGLR 1081.

Fundamental Human Rights and Freedoms guaranteed by this Constitution." In that regard, as provided by Article 33(1) of the Constitution, where a person alleges that a provision of the Constitution on the fundamental human rights and freedoms has been, or is being or is likely to be contravened in relation to him, that person can apply to the High Court for redress.

These two provisions, therefore, oust the jurisdiction of any court, be it the Court of Appeal or the Supreme Court from entertaining at first instance any matter the substance of which is human rights.[28]

However where a matter before a court is not a human rights matter but in the course of the proceedings an issue bothering on the enforcement of human rights arises, the court will be fortified to deal with it and the matter ought not to be referred to the High Court. Recently, the Supreme Court has proclaimed that, notwithstanding the exclusive jurisdiction given to the High Court in the enforcement of human rights matters, where the matter albeit a human rights matter is of greater public interest, the court shall have the jurisdiction in that regard. This was the holding in the case of *Adjei Ampofo v Accra Metropolitan Assembly & Attorney General.*[29] By virtue of Article 130 of the Constitution, 1992 the Supreme Court shall be the only court with jurisdiction to interpret and enforce the Constitution. This means that, even where the High Court is deciding on a human rights matter but the matter raises an issue of constitutional interpretation, the High Court must stay proceedings and refer the matter to the Supreme Court.[30]

## Making an Application to the High Court for the Enforcement of Human Right

The procedure by which a person could seek the enforcement of his right is governed by Article 33(1) of the Constitution, 1992 and Order 67 of the High Court Civil Procedure Rules, 2004 (C.I. 47). Under Order 67 rule 1, a person who seeks redress in respect of the enforcement of any of the human rights in relation to that person under Article 33 must do so by way of an application to the High Court.

---

28 *Edusei v Attorney General* [1997-98] 2 GLR 1; *Joseph Sam v Attorney-General* [2000] SCGLR 305.

29 [2007-08] SCGLR 611

30 Article 130(2) of the Constitution 1992; Republic v High Court, Accra Ex Parte Commission on Human Rights and Administrative Justice (Anane Interested Party) [2007-2008] SCGLR 213.

## Locus Standi

An application to the High Court pursuant to Article 33 of the 1992 Constitution will not be entertained by the High Court unless the applicant is the victim. This requirement is reflected clearly in the wording of the Article that *"**Where a person** alleges that a provision of this Constitution on the fundamental human rights and freedom has been, or is being or is likely to be contravened **in relation to him**…"*. Busy bodies cannot therefore, purport to seek an enforcement of human rights. The enforcement under Article 33 is therefore, personified. The person within Article 33 is not limited to only natural persons but also covers artificial or juristic persons like companies, partnerships and political parties in Ghana. As provided for under the Interpretation Act,[31] a 'person' includes *"a body corporate, whether corporation aggregate or corporation sole and an unincorporated body of persons as well as an individual."*[32]

In *Nana Adjei Ampofo v AG*, the Plaintiff was not the victim of human rights abuse however, the Supreme Court exercised jurisdiction in the case on the basis of the significant public interest issue that was raised in the case. It stands to reason that in appropriate cases hinging on public policy and public interest, the Supreme Court will make pronouncement seeking the enforcement of rights of others although the suit was brought by a person not the subject of human rights abuse.

## Mode of making application

The application for the enforcement of human rights under Article 33 shall be made by a motion, which is supported by an affidavit and signed by the applicant himself or his lawyer detailing the following particulars:

    a. The full name and address for service of the applicant and the lawyer of the applicant;
    b. The facts upon which the applicant relies

31 Interpretation Act, 2009 (Act 792).
32 See also the Supreme Court case of New Patriotic Party v Attorney-General (31st December case) wherein the Supreme court noted that Article 33 of the Constitution availed artificial persons such as political parties.

c. The relief or remedy sought by the applicant and the ground on which the applicant seeks the relief or remedy; and

d. The full name and address for service of any person directly affected by the application.[33]

A copy of the application shall also be served on the attorney-general and any such person at the direction of the court.[34]

## Time for Making the Application

The application must be submitted to the High Court within six months of the occurrence of the alleged contravention or three months of the applicant becoming aware that the contravention is occurring or it is likely to occur.[35] Notice of the application must be served on the Attorney General and all parties named in the application if the court finds same desirable.[36]

## Response to the Application

Within twenty-one days of service of notice of the application on the Attorney General or any other person affected by the application, the Attorney-General or that person shall file an affidavit in answer to the application. The respondent must state facts and law, if any, on which the respondent relies in support of his case.[37]

Where a party seeks to amend, the party must seek leave from the court and upon grant amend the application or file supplementary affidavit within seven days of the grant of the leave.

## Setting Down the Application for Hearing

Within twenty-one days of the service of an affidavit in reply to the application the applicant shall set down the application for hearing and he shall give notice of same to the other parties in the proceedings.[38] During

33 Order 67 rule 2(1) of C.I. 47.
34 Order 67 rule 2(2) of C.I. 47.
35 Order 67 rule 3 (1) of C.I. 47.
36 Order 67 rule 3(2) & (3) of C.I. 47.
37 Order 67 rule 4 of C.I. 47.
38 Order 67 Rule 5als.

the hearing of the application a party may call any witness in support of the application and likewise, the court is also allowed to call any witness it deems relevant to testify.[39]

## Reliefs Granted

In securing the enforcement of its human rights jurisdiction, the High Court may issue directions and orders in the nature of *habeas corpus, certiorari, mandamus, prohibition and quo warranto* as it may consider appropriate.[40]

Any person dissatisfied with any of the orders and or directions issued by the High Court may appeal to the Court of Appeal and has a further right of appeal to the Supreme Court.[41]

## Emerging Issues in the Recognition and Enforcement of Fundamental Human Rights in Ghana
## Judicial Pragmatism in the Enforcement of Privacy Rights

Following Anas Aremeyaw Anas' expose #No. 12, there has been series of debates on his method of getting information to advance his cause. Without delving into a discussion on issues of entrapment which is a primary subject regarding the extraction of information, it suffices to say that, there has been a new breath into the enforcement of privacy rights guaranteed under Article 18(2) of the Constitution 1992. The Article frowns upon interference with the privacy of a person's home, property, correspondence or communication *'except in accordance with law and as may be necessary in a free and democratic society for pubic safety or the economic well-being of the country, for the protection of health or morals, for the prevention of disorder or crime or for the protection of the rights or freedoms of others.'*

The Supreme Court in two recent decisions, *Abena Pokua v Agricultural Development Bank*[42] and *Raphael Cubagee v Michael Yeboa Asare & Ors*[43] have affirmed the privacy rights of individuals under Article 18(2) of the Constitution. The Court has reasoned that a person cannot without the consent of another secretly take recordings of communication of that other and use same as evidence in court.

39 Order 67 rule 6 of C.I. 47.
40 Order 67 rule 8 of C.I. 47.
41 Order 67 rule 9 of C.I. 47.
42 Suit No. CA/J4/31/ 2015 dated 20th December 2017.
43 Case No. J6/04/2017 SC dated 28th February 2018.

In *Raphael Cubagee v Michael Yeboah*, in the course of testifying in a land case before the District Magistrate, the plaintiff sought to tender in evidence audio recording of a telephone conversation he had had with one another wherein that other person (a Rev. Minister) sought to corroborate the case of the plaintiff. Counsel for the defendant objected to the tendering on the basis that same was clandestinely procured, which was in violation of the privacy rights of the Rev. Minister. In consequence, the court referred the matter to the Supreme Court to decide whether the secrete recording was a violation of privacy rights under Article 18(2) of the Constitution and whether same could be tendered in evidence. The Supreme Court speaking through Pwamang JSC held that the said secret recording was in breach of the privacy rights and same was inadmissible as evidence. In upholding the privacy rights under Article 18(2) of the Constitution, 1992 Pwamang JSC maintained that the essence of the constitutional guarantee of the privacy rights of the individual was to protect '*the individual against unwarranted intrusion, scrutiny and publicity and guarantees his control over intrusions into his private sphere.*' The Court further pointed out that the individual may decide the extent to which he will allow such interference by stating that '*[W]hen a person talks on telephone to another, the conversation is meant to be oral communication since if the speaker wanted the speech in a permanent form he cold elect to write it down or record and send to the other person…It would be wrong for the person at the other end to assume that the speaker has waived his rights of privacy and consented to him recording the conversation and rendering it in a permanent state.*'

It needs mention that the court did not lay out a blanket rule. A judge has the discretion to assess whether the evidence procured in breach of Article 18(2) ought to be admitted nonetheless by considering the nature of the rights that has been violated, the manner and degree of the violation, the gravity of the crime being tried, the manner in which the offence was committed as well as the severity of the sentence which the offence attracts.

## The Right Of Every Accused Person to all Evidence and Other Materials the Prosecution Decides to Rely on in a Criminal Case or in the Possession of the Prosecution Relevant to the Case

In securing the enforcement of fair trial in criminal cases in Ghana, the Supreme Court has adopted the policy of disclosures that exist in civil suits in Ghana. In civil cases parties at the case management stage are enjoined to make disclosures and exchange documents that are necessary to facilitate the trial and avoid surprises. There has however, not been any judicial pronouncement on this in criminal trials despite the adequate fair trial provisions in the Constitution.[44] However, in the recent Supreme Court case of *The Republic v Eugene Baffoe-Bonnie and 4 Ors,*[45] the Supreme Court adopted the approach in civil cases and concluded that accused persons are also entitled to all evidence that the prosecution intends to rely on in the course of the trial. This in the view of the court is essential to allowing such accused persons to mount adequate defence and thereby satisfying the right to fair trial.

In fortifying the above decision of the Supreme Court, there has been a recent 2018 practice direction wherein her ladyship the Chief Justice has directed that the following materials must be disclosed by the prosecutor to the accused[46]:

> a. Copy of the Charge Sheet/Indictment
>
> b. Copy of the Facts of the Prosecution's case
>
> c. Copies of Statements made by the accused person before commencement of trial (such as Cautioned Statement, Charge Statement, Statutory Statement as well as any further Statements made by the accused person before trial commences).
>
> d. Copies of all Witness Statements made to the Police and other law enforcement or investigative bodies by persons who may or may not be called upon to testify for the prosecution at the trial.
>
> e. Copies of any documents in possession of the prosecution which are relevant to the case and which the prosecution may or may not tender at the trial.
>
> f. Photographs of any real evidence (objects) in possession of the prosecution which are relevant to the case and which the prosecution may or may not tender at the trial, such as guns, cutlasses, knifes, etc.
>
> g. Copies of any other materials in possession of the Prosecution which are relevant to the case including audio, video and other electronic recordings as well as any unused materials which may assist the accused person in the preparation of his defence.

---

44 Articles 19 and 14 of the 1992 Constitution.

45 Suit No. J1/06/2018, judgment given on 6th June 2018.

46 An accused has been interpreted to include the lawyer for the accused.

h. Copies of any exculpatory evidence in possession of the Police and other law enforcement or investigative bodies (the prosecution is under an obligation to inquire from the relevant law enforcement or investigative bodies the existence of such evidence, procure and preserve same for disclosure

i. Further that without prejudice to paragraph h, the court on its own motion or on an application by the accused (defence), may order that any statement, document, object or material in possession of the Police or other law enforcement or investigative bodies that is relevant to the case but which the prosecution has not disclosed.

Whilst enjoying disclosures from the prosecution, the accused person is also without prejudice to the presumption of innocence and also for purposes of case management to disclose the names and addresses of all witnesses he expects to call should the Court call upon him to enter into his defence at the close of case for the prosecution. Further, where before making disclosure the Prosecution requires an undertaking of non-disclosure by the accused person for the protection of third parties or the public interest, the accused person shall provide such undertaking before the disclosure is made.

Again, the accused shall indicate if there are any witnesses he expects to call by use of witnesses summons to enable the summons to be issued on time and where the accused intends to put forward as a defence a plea of *alibi*, the Accused shall give timely notice of the *alibi*.

These disclosures enjoined on both the prosecution and accused to be made before a criminal trial furthers the right to fair trial of all accused persons and it is a welcoming step in our criminal justice system.

**Conclusion and Reflections**

This paper has attempted a cursory overview of the human rights regime in Ghana. It considered the courts with jurisdiction over human right cases, the enforcement procedures and some emerging rights that have received firm pronouncement by the Supreme Court.

The naturalist's perspective of human rights is very operational in Ghana and that the courts will at all times seek the enforcement of any right that satisfies the tests of being inherent in a democracy and intended to secure the freedom and dignity of man.

The entitlements of these rights as noted enjoins the respect of the rights of others and as the popular aphorism goes, where one's right ends, another's begin. It should not be forgotten however, that some of these rights, especially the economic rights may be positive in character. That is, their enjoyment may be contingent on the availability of resources. In that regard, the courts will be slow to make them justiciable. However, as demonstrated the courts should be ready to greatly influence political decisions as the rights of individuals cannot be toyed with on the altar of politics.

# 4

# OVER SIXTY YEARS OF BAIL UNDER THE GHANAIAN CRIMINAL JUSTICE SYSTEM

## Francisca Kusi-Appiah

### Abstract

Laws on bail in Ghana were developed out of English statutes and policies. Ghana practices the adversarial system of criminal justice system and the accused person is presumed to be innocent until proven guilty. The right to freedom of movement is enshrined in the Constitution of Ghana. This paper analyzes existing laws and the decisions given by the courts in Ghana over the past sixty years of independence and how it has affected the fundamental human rights of Ghanaians. The 1992 Constitution has provisions, which recognizes the personal liberty of every individual as well as the fundamental rights of every person when arrested and detained. The provisions under the 1992 Constitution make bail available when there is likely to be a delay in the judicial process. The Criminal Procedure Code, 1960 (Act 30) makes mention of bail and gives certain conditions upon, which bail may or may not be given. Act 30, as amended, gives discretion to the court to either grant or refuse an application for bail. The examination of Constitutional and statutory provisions, as well as case law in Ghana, for the past sixty (60) years of independence, indicates that the fundamental rights of Ghanaians is paramount but the Constitutional presumption of innocence does not import an automatic right to bail and that bail is discretionary. However, in the case of police enquiry bail, there is a duty on the police to grant bail after detention of forty-eight hours or take the accused person to the court for any extension of the detention.

## Introduction

Justice as simply defined by the Osborn's Concise Dictionary[1] is *the upholding of rights and the punishment of wrongs, by the law.* Accordingly, a criminal justice system could be said to be the upholding of rights and the punishment of wrongs under the criminal laws and procedures of a state such as Ghana.

Ghana practices the adversarial system of criminal justice system, where the person who asserts or alleges the commission of a crime by another must prove beyond reasonable doubt or admit his guilt but until that is done, the accused person is presumed to be innocent.[2] The criminal justice system in Ghana has various stages, which start right from arrest, detention, bail, trial and judgment. This paper examines bail as a stage in the administration of criminal justice in Ghana, for the past sixty years of independence, for the benefit of advancing the development of the administration of the criminal justice in Ghana.

Right from creation man was given the freedom to move about without any restrictions over all he saw.[3] However, with time the freedom was gradually restricted to enhance a congenial environment for man to live peacefully with his or her neighbour. This eventually gave way to the creation of rules to guide and guard the behaviour and activities of all men. This confirms the statement that *law is born from despair of human nature.*[4]

Previously under the common law, whenever a suspect was arrested, he was detained till he was either convicted or discharged of the crime he was accused of. However, it became necessary after subsequent instances where men who were acquitted could not be compensated enough after the embarrassment of being detained, to allow the accused person to go back home. To add to that, under the principle of natural justice, it was necessary to allow the accused persons to go home and prepare their defences in order to arrive at a fair and

---

1 Edited by Leslie Rutherford and Sheila Bone (8th Edition)
2 1992 Constitution, Article 19(2)(c)
3 Genesis Chapter 2:19, New King's James Bible
4 José Ortega y Gasset, 1883-1955, W.H. Auden and Louis Kronemberger, The Viking Book of Aphorisms, 1962, *The Quotable Lawyer*

justifiable decision. For as the saying goes, *"it is better to allow ninety-nine guilty ones to go scot-free than to convict an innocent soul".*[5] During the early civilization, the principle of arrest and detention became necessary to ensure that the accused persons were available for trial and would not escape from the grips of the law.[6] Laws on bail in Ghana were developed out of English statutes and policies. During the colonial period, Ghana relied on the bail system that had been developed in England hundred years earlier. When Ghana was declared a Republic in 1960, Ghana developed her own bail laws and policies, which were closely parallel to the English tradition.

This paper analyzes existing laws and the decisions given by the courts in Ghana and indicates any changes made to the bail system in Ghana within the last sixty years of Ghana's independence and how it has affected the fundamental human rights of Ghanaians.

The 1992 Constitution has provisions, which recognizes the personal liberty of every individual as well as the fundamental rights of every person when arrested and detained.[7] The provisions under the 1992 Constitution make bail available when there is likely to be a delay in the judicial process. The Criminal Procedure Code, 1960 (Act 30) makes mention of bail and gives certain conditions upon, which bail may or may not be given. Act 30, as amended, gives discretion to the court to either grant or refuse an application for bail.

### Bail in Ghana's Criminal Justice System

Bail is defined as *a security such as cash or a bond, especially security required by a court for the release of a prisoner who must appear at a future time or the process by which a person is released from custody either on the undertaking of a surety or on his or her own recognizance.*[8] The Osborn's Concise Law Dictionary defines bail as *the release from custody of officers of the law or the court of an accused or convicted person, who undertakes to subsequently surrender to custody.* These definitions encapsulate bail before trial, during trial and pending appeal.

5 J.B. Lippincott Co., "William Blackstone, Commentaries on the Laws of England (1760)", Philadelphia, 1893, page 358

6 R.G. Collinwood, The Idea of History: Epilegomena: 5 - History and Freedom, paragraph 315-6

7 Article 4

8 Black Law's Dictionary (8th Ed, 2004), page 426

Prior to Ghana's independence in 1957, English Laws governed Ghana (then known as the Gold Coast) as a British Colony. The common law and equity was received in the Gold Coast through the reception clause of the Supreme court ordinance of 1876, which provided that the common law, doctrines of equity and the statutes of general application, which were in force in England on 24th of July 1874, shall be in force within the jurisdiction of the Supreme Court.

Therefore, just before the independence of Ghana, the courts were given the discretionary to grant bail whether the offence was a misdemeanour or a felony.[9] However, if the granting of the bail will be against public policy, the courts can refuse to grant bail but bail cannot be withheld as punishment. In the granting of bail, the courts also had the mandate to review the accused person's previous conviction, although this is in conflict with the principle of presuming the accused innocent until proven guilty.

After independence, the first Constitution of Ghana[10] never mentioned or made any provision on the fundamental human rights of Ghana and most importantly did not talk of the right to bail after arrest. The second Constitution, which came into operation on the 1st of July 1960, Ghana's Republican Day, never made any express provisions on fundamental human rights and specifically on the right to bail. The only provision made was under Article 13, which required the President of Ghana to make a declaration to uphold the fundamental principles of the Constitution. The same Article empowered the President to make restrictions on the freedom and rights of Ghanaians as long as it was geared toward preservation of public order, morality or health. The case of Re Akoto,[11] throws more light on Article 13. In Re Akoto, the appellants were arrested and placed in detention under an Order by the Governor-General and signed on his behalf by the Minister of Interior under section 2 of the Preventive Detention Act, 1958.[12] Their application to the High Court for writs of habeas corpus as subjiciendum was refused. They appealed and the Supreme Court held that:

*"It will be observed that Article 13(1) is in the form of a provisional declaration*

---

9 Civil Procedure (4 Edw. 3, 10), Justices of the Peace Act 1361 (34 Edw. 3, c. 1), the Felony Act (1 Ric. 3, c. 3), as cited in Okoe v the Republic (1976) I GLR @p 85; R. v. Phillips (1947) 32 Cr.App.R. 47 at p. 48, C.C.A.

10 The Ghana (Constitution) Order in Council, 1957

11 (1961) GLR 523

12 No. 17 of 1958

*by the president and is in no way part of the general law of Ghana. In the other parts of the Constitution where a duty is imposed by the word 'shall' is often used, but throughout the declaration, the word used is 'should'. In our view the declaration merely represents the goal, which every President must pledge himself to attempt to achieve. It does not represent a legal requirement, which can be enforced by the courts".*

From the above, Article 13 only placed a moral obligation on every President and did not create any legally enforceable obligation. However, after the enactment of the Criminal Procedure Code, 1960,[13] the issue of bail was well provided for in section 96, which stated that:

> *(1) When a person, other than a person accused of an offence punishable with death appears or is brought before any court on any process or after being arrested without a warrant, and is prepared at any time or at any stage of the proceedings or after conviction pending an appeal to give bail, he may in the discretion of the Court be released upon his entering in the manner hereinafter provided into a bond, with or without a surety or sureties, conditioned for his appearance before that court or some other Court at the time and place mentioned in the bond.*
>
> *(2) The amount of bail shall be fixed with due regard to the circumstances of the case and shall not be excessive*
>
> *(3) Notwithstanding anything in this section or in section 15 the High Court or a Circuit Court may in any case direct that any person be admitted to bail or that the bail required by a District Court or police officer be reduced.*

Therefore, all accused persons irrespective of their crimes were entitled to bail apart from those whose offence could be punishable by death. The provision also indicates that bail can be granted by a police officer or by the courts, during the proceedings of the case or after conviction pending appeal. Following from the provisions in the Criminal Code, the grant of bail to persons in custody before trial in cases of delay became subject to the provisions of Article 15(3)(b) and (4) of the 1969 Constitution of Ghana, which provided that:

> *"15(3) Any person who is arrested, restricted or detained…*

13 Act 30; became effective on the 12th of January 1961.

*(b) upon reasonable suspicion of his having committed, or being about to commit, a criminal offence under the law of Ghana, and who is not released, shall be brought before a Court within twenty-four hours.*

*(4) Where a person arrested, restricted or detained in any circumstance as is mentioned in paragraph (b) of the immediately preceding clause is not tried within a reasonable time, then, without prejudice to any further proceedings that may be brought against him, he shall be released either unconditionally or upon reasonable condition, including in particular such conditions as are reasonably necessary to ensure that he appears at a later date for trial or for proceedings preliminary to trial."*

The Constitutional provision is supreme to the provisions in the Criminal Code as expressed by Justice Taylor J (as he then was) in the case of OKOE v THE REPUBLIC,[14] where he stated that:

*"...Once there is an unreasonable delay in prosecuting the case, then section 96 of Act 30 (as amended) is in my view inapplicable and Article 15(3)(b) and (4) of the Constitution, 1969 becomes applicable and in such a situation, bail in all cases must be given subject only to the conditions prescribed in the Articles."*

In 1975, the Criminal Procedure Code (Amendment) Decree[15] by section 2 amended the section 96 of the Criminal Procedure Code, 1960[16] by substituting a new section 96, which reads:

*96. (1) Subject to this section, a Court may grant bail to a person who appears or is brought before it on a process or after being arrested without warrant, and who*

*(a) is prepared at any time or at any stage of the proceedings or after conviction pending an appeal to give bail, and*

*(b) enters into a bond in the manner hereinafter provided with or without sureties, conditioned for his appearance before that Court*

14 (1976) I GLR p 80 at 95-96
15 N.R.C.D. 309
16 Act 30

*or some other Court at the time and place mentioned in the bond.*
*(2) Notwithstanding anything in subsection (1) of this section or in section 15, but subject to the following provisions of this section, the High Court or a Circuit Court may direct that a person be admitted to bail or that the bail required by a District Court or police officer be reduced.*
*(3) The amount and conditions of bail shall be fixed with due regard to the circumstances of the case and shall not be excessive or harsh.*
*(4) A Court shall not withhold or withdraw bail merely as a punishment.*
*(5) A Court shall refuse to grant bail if it is satisfied that the defendant*
> *(a) may not appear to stand trial, or*
> *(b) may interfere with any witness or the evidence, or in any way hamper police investigations, or*
> *(c) may commit a further offence when on bail, or*
> *(d) is charged with an offence punishable by imprisonment exceeding six months which is alleged to have been committed while the defendant was on bail.*

*(6) In considering whether it is likely that the defendant may not appear to stand trial the Court shall take into account the following considerations:*
> *(a) the nature of the accusation,*
> *(b) the nature of the evidence in support of the accusation,*
> *(c) the severity of the punishment which conviction will entail,*
> *(d) whether the defendant, having been released on bail on a previous occasion, has willfully failed to comply with the conditions of any recognisance entered into by him on that occasion,*
> *(e) whether or not the defendant has a fixed place of abode in Ghana, and is gainfully employed,*
> *(f) whether the sureties are independent, of good character and of sufficient means.*

*(7) A Court shall refuse to grant bail*
> *(a) in a case of acts of terrorism, treason, subversion, murder, robbery, hijacking, piracy or escape from lawful custody, or*
> *(b) where a person is being held for extradition to a foreign country."*

From the above, section 96(1) gives discretion to any court to admit any person who appears or is brought before it and who is prepared to give bail and to enter into recognizance with or without sureties as is directed by the court. This provision has nothing to do with delay in the trial, which is covered by Article 15(4) of the 1969 Constitution. It would seem, therefore, that section 96(1) merely stated the power of the courts to grant bail to persons brought before them while section 96(2) confirmed the common law discretionary power of the High Court. A comparison between the previous provisions on bail under the Criminal Procedure Code (Act 30) and the amendment made under the NRCD 309 reflects the identical similarities of the first three provisions except where NRCD 309 made express provisions on issues to be considered before the grant of bail as well as circumstances under which bail should be refused.

The third Republic gave birth to the third Republic Constitution of 1979 and Article 21(3)(b) and (4)(a) of the 1979 Constitution substantially re-enacted the provisions of Article 15(3)(b) and (4) of the 1969 Constitution. The 1979 provision read as:

> 21 (3) A person who is arrested, restricted or detained,
> (a) for the purposes of bringing him before a Court in execution of the order of a Court or
> (b) upon reasonable suspicion of his having committed, or being about to commit, a criminal offence under the law of Ghana, and who is not released, shall be brought before a Court within twenty-four hours.
> (4) Where a person arrested, restricted or detained in any circumstance as is mentioned in paragraph (b) of clause (3) of this article is not tried within a reasonable time, then, without prejudice to any further proceedings that may be brought against him:
> (a) he shall be released either unconditionally or upon reasonable conditions, including in particular such conditions as are reasonably necessary to ensure that he appears at a later date for trial or for proceedings preliminary to trial

Reading the provisions of Act 30 and the 1979 Constitution on bail demonstrate that a court was to refuse bail, in murder cases and under some circumstances, except in the cases of unreasonable delay of the trial of the accused person.

The current prevailing constitutional provisions can be found in the 1992 Constitution of Ghana. Article 11(4) of the 1992 Constitution acknowledges the fact that all existing laws prior to the coming into force of the 1992 Constitution and are not contrary to the provisions of the 1992 constitution, shall continue to have effect. This means that the Criminal Procedure Code as an existing law prior to the promulgation of the 1992 Constitution still has effect as long as it does not contradict the provision of the 1992 Constitution. The 1992 Constitution contains unambiguous protection for accused persons in the pretrial and trial stages of the criminal process. Article 19(2) (c) articulates the age-old common law presumption of the innocence of the accused. In addition, Article 14 embodies a direct duty to grant bail in specific situation. That is when a person is not tried within a reasonable time.

Article 14(1) and (3) operate on the premise that every person is generally entitled to his liberty except in specified cases and that even where a person's liberty is restricted that person must be produced before a court within forty-eight hours or regain his liberty. Article 14(1), 14(3) and Article 19(2)(c) of the 1992 Constitution provide a constitutional presumption of grant of bail in the areas falling outside the courts' direct duty to the grant of bail under Article 14(4). However, this presumption is rebuttable. Any alternative interpretation would lead to a conclusion that every accused person has an automatic right to bail under the Constitution.

Aside Article 14(4) of the Constitution and section 96(7) of the Criminal Procedure Code, the presumption of the grant of bail retains judicial discretion in the matter of bails. However, the exercise of this discretion remains fettered by other relevant provisions of our law and this is where the other provisions of section 96(1) of the code fall into place.

The combined reading of the 1992 Constitution and the Criminal Procedure Code raise the following questions:

Whether the Constitutional presumption of innocence rooted in Article 19(2) (c) of the 1992 Constitution does not import an automatic right to bail.

Whether the constitutional duty of the court under Article 14(4) of the Constitution to grant bail to the accused if he is not tried within a reasonable time is applicable irrespective of the nature of the accusation or the severity of the punishment upon conviction.

Whether cases falling outside the direct duty to grant bail under Article 14(4), gives a constitutional presumption of grant of bail drawn from the spirit of the language of Article 14(1) and (3) and 19(2)(c) in further protection of persons charge with offences in situations which do not mandate the grant of bail.

## Kinds of Bail

Analysis of the 1992 Constitution and the Criminal Procedure Code reveal that there are three kinds of bail in Ghana, namely: police enquiry bail, bail pending or during trial, and bail pending or during appeal.

## Police Enquiry Bail

Police enquiry bail, as stated by A. N. E. Amissah,[17] arises when the police, without a warrant, has arrested a person and the investigations are likely not to be completed within forty-eight hours. The police must either produce him or her before a court or grant him bail to appear at some later specified date at the police station for the investigations to continue.

Section 15 of the Criminal Procedure Code, on the 12th of January 1961, provided that:

> *(1) If any person has been taken into custody without a warrant for an offence other than an offence punishable with death, the officer in charge of the police station.... shall at once enquire into the case, and if, when the enquiry is completed there is no sufficient reason to believe that the person has committed any offence he shall be released forthwith.*
>
> *(2) If upon the completion of the enquiry, there is reason to believe that the person arrested has committed an offence and, if the offence does not appear to be of serious nature, the officer may, and shall, if it does not appear practicable to bring such a person before an appropriate court within twenty-four hours after he was taken into custody, release the person on his executing a bond, with or without sureties for a reasonable amount, to appear before a court at a time and place named in the bond.*

Deductions made from the above indicate that if the offence is not punishable by death then the police officer can after his enquiries if sufficient reason is not found that the accused committed the crime for which he was

17 Criminal Procedure in Ghana, Sedco Publishing (1st ed., 1985)

brought there, release the accused. However, if sufficient reason is found that the accused person committed the offence for which he is accused of, the police officer in charge may executive a bond with or without sureties when appearance before the court within twenty-four hours seem impossible. The same applies where enquiries is not completed but the bond executed must include the times within which the accused person is to report at the police station unless the accused person receives a notice in writing from the Officer in charge that his attendance is no longer required. A bond under section 15(3) is to be treated as if the bond had been entered in, in a court of law conditional for the accused person's appearance.

The case of DASWANI v COMMISSIONER OF POLICE,[18] discusses obligation of sureties under a bail bond and circumstances under which obligations under a bail bond may be discharged. In that case, Daswani, the appellant appealed against the decision of a circuit court whereby he forfeited the sum under a bond in which he stood as surety, for his failure to secure the appearance of the principal at a time when he was required by the police. It was his contention that since the police failed to specify another date on the bond at the time when the principal party appeared before them, that in itself amounted to discharge of the bond. The respondent, on the other hand, maintained that it was not necessary to specify a new date on the bond, and that it was only when a police officer wrote to indicate the principal's attendance was no longer required that the bond could become discharged.

Justice Sowah (as he then was) stated that a bail bond like a civil bond is a contract under seal, and for the bond to be enforceable against the obligees or the principal party, any conditions (that is the other dates for reporting at the police station after the first appearance) precedent must be fulfilled. In the present case, failure on the part of the police to state another date for the appearance of the principal party discharged the surety from his obligations under the bond, and such failure was a defence to any action, which might be brought to enforce the obligation under the bond.

The above shows that the Police Officer in charge has been granted a lot of discretionary powers to determine what is "sufficient reason" of the commission of the offence of which that person is being accused of but the date of appearance and any another essential obligation have to be stated in the bond to prevent any confusion when sureties are lost due to breach of the conditions attached to the execute bond.

18 (1964) No. 2 GLR p. 54

On the 14th December, 1973, the passage of NRCD 235 amended section 15 of the Criminal Procedure Code, 1960 (Act 30), substituted the following:

> *(1) A person taken into custody without a warrant in connection with any offence shall be released from custody not later than forty-eight hours after his arrest unless he is earlier brought before a court of competent jurisdiction.*
>
> *(2) A person so taken into custody may at any time whether before or after the expiration of the said period be required to enter into a bond with or without sureties for a reasonable amount to appear before such court or at such police station or place and at such time as may be stated in the bond.*
>
> *(3) Any such bond may be enforced as if it were a bond executed by order of a court and conditioned for the appearance of the said person before a court.*

This provision was almost like that of the Criminal Procedure Code but for the fact that the time within which a person arrested without warrant could be lawfully held in police custody before arrangement of such a person before a court of law was increased to forty-eight (48) hours or two days instead of the twenty-four (24) or a day. In addition, this new provision did not restrict powers of the police to only offences not punishable by death but to all offences but the police retained their discretionary powers in matters concerning reasonability of sureties.

NRCD 309 of 3rd January, 1975 repealed certain previous provisions on bail and section 96(2) and (3) of the Criminal Procedure Code, 1960 stipulated that irrespective of the police's ability to execute bonds based on sureties, due regard should be given to the circumstances of the case and that the sureties shall not be neither harsh nor excessive. But the question is: 'who determines what is excessive?' Here recourse might be had to the courts under subsection 2 where the court can reduce the bail granted by a police officer.

After twelve years, the amendment made by NRCD 235 to section 15 of the Criminal Procedure Code was further amended on the 1st of April, 1977 to the effect that: Section 15 of the Criminal Procedure Code, 1960 (Act 30) as amended, is hereby further amended as follows –

(a) by the substitution for subsection (1) thereof, of the following new subsection – Section 15 'Holding In Custody of Persons Arrested Without Warrant – (1) A person taken into custody not later than thirty days after his arrest unless he is earlier brought before a court of competent jurisdiction"

(b) by the insertion at the end thereof, of the following new subsection – "(4) Section 96 of the Criminal Procedure Code, 1960 (Act 30)(which relates to bail) shall not apply to a person held in custody under this section."

The above provision depicts that the number of days that is the twenty-four hours (a day), which an accused person should have been brought before a court of law or released either conditionally or unconditionally has been increased to thirty (30) days. The major argument in support of this increment is to ensure that the accused person is always available to assist the police with their investigations. Article 14 of the 1992 Constitution of Ghana, the supreme law of the land, on the protection of personal liberty, clearly states that

> "14(3) A person who is arrested, restricted or detained –
> (a) for the purpose of bringing him before a court in execution of an order of a court; or
> (b) upon reasonable suspicion of his having committed or being about to commit a criminal offence under the laws of Ghana, and who is not released, shall be brought before a court within forty-eight hours after the arrest, restriction or detention.
> (4) Where a person arrested, restricted or detained under paragraph (a) or (b) of clause (3) of this article is not tried within a reasonable time, then, without prejudice to any further proceedings that may be brought against him, he shall be released, either unconditionally or upon reasonable conditions, including in particular conditions reasonably necessary to ensure that he appears at a later date for trial or for proceedings preliminary to trial."

This places a duty on the police officer, who caused the arrest or who was in charge of the station at the time when the accused was brought into the custody of the station to either release the accused conditionally or unconditionally reasonably necessary to cause the appearance of the accused person at a later date for trial or for proceedings preliminary to trial. These constitutional provisions fueled the enactment of Act 633 of 12th August 2002, which amended section 15 of previous decrees in the Criminal Procedure on bail. Act 633 provided that:

*The principal enactment is amended in section 15 as follows:*

> *(a) in subsection (1) by the deletion of "thirty days" and the insertion of "forty-eight hours", and*
> *(b) by the repeal of subsection (4).*

Section 16 of Act 30 requires that an officer in charge of a police station gives a monthly report, to the nearest District Magistrate, of persons arrested without warrant within the jurisdiction of the police station, whether or not bail was granted, as long as the arrested persons were not subsequently charged with an offence. Here the District Magistrate is to act as a check on the Police to ensure that the human rights of accused persons are respected.

## Bail Before Trial Or During Trial

The 1960 Criminal Procedure Code (Act 30), in section 96 provided that *"when any person, other than a person accused of an offence punishable with death appears or is brought **before any court** on any process or after being arrested without a warrant, and is prepared at any time or at any stage of the proceedings ..., he may in the discretion of **the Court** be released upon his entering in the manner hereinafter provided into a bond, with or without a surety or sureties, conditioned for his appearance **before that Court or some other Court** at the time and place mentioned in the bond."*

The 1969 Constitution in Article 15(4) provided that *"Where a person arrested, restricted or detained in any circumstance ... is not tried within a reasonable time, then without prejudice to any further proceedings that my be brought against him, he shall be released either unconditionally or upon reasonable conditions, including in particular such conditions as are reasonably necessary to ensure that he appears at a latter date or for proceedings preliminary to trial".*

Article 14(1)(a) & (g) of the 1992 Constitution provides that *"Every person shall be entitled to his personal liberty and no person shall be deprived of his personal liberty except in execution of an order of a court, upon reasonable suspicion of his having committed or being about to commit a criminal offence under the laws of Ghana."*

However, Article 14 (3) of the 1992 Constitution states that if a person is arrested, restricted or detained and is not released within forty-eight hours, that person has to be brought before a court of competent jurisdiction. Under Article 14(4), the court may release an arrested, restricted or detained person, who is not tried within a reasonable time, either unconditionally or upon reasonable conditions, without prejudice to any further proceedings that may be brought against him.

It was not until 1971 that the courts dealt with cases pertaining to bail during trial because, as earlier indicated, the first two constitutions of Ghana did not expressly make provisions for the grant of bail.

To buttress the point further is the case of GYAKYE and Another v. THE REPUBLIC.[19] In this case, Coussey J (as he then was) sitting as a High Court Judge in Sekondi where the applicants were arrested, and charged with murder contrary to section 46 of the criminal code, 1960 (Act 29) stated that under Article 15(4) of the Constitution, 1969, where a person is arrested, restricted, detained in any circumstance as mentioned in paragraph (b) of the immediate preceding clause, is not tried within a reasonable time, shall be released either unconditionally or upon a reasonable conditions, including in particular such conditions as are reasonably necessary to ensure that he appears at a later date for trial or for proceedings preliminary to trial. The learned judge further held that since the accused persons had been held in custody for a long period and yet there was no indication as to when their trial will start, trial had not taken place within a reasonable time. Therefore, he was compelled with the spirit and letter of the Constitution to allow the applicants bail.

Thus, bail in case of murder was not to be granted under the Criminal Procedure Code but where there seem to be any unreasonable delay then the accused under the 1969 Constitution was entitled to be granted bail.[20]

Five years after the judgement in the case of Gyakye, another issue on bail was address in a new murder case of ABIAM v. THE REPUBLIC.[21] The facts are that the applicant, who was a 58-year old man placed in custody pending the hearing of a charge of attempted murder preferred against him brought an application for bail on grounds of ill health but the application for bail was challenged on the grounds that the offence of attempt murder could be

19 (1971) 2 GLR 280
20 Article title "Bail in Murder cases" published in the Review of the Ghana Law (1987-88) Vol. XVI p. 225
21 (1976) 1 GLR p.270

included in the offence of murder, in respect of which the Criminal Procedure Code, 1960 (Act 30) section 96 as amended by the Criminal Procedure Code (Amendment) Decree, 1975 (N.R.C.D. 309) section 2, mandatorily prohibited the granting of bail.

Mensah Boison J. (as he then was) held that *"(1) the mandatory provision against the granting of bail was in respect of the offence of murder and not attempted murder but the offence of attempted murder could not be included in that of murder... To add to that the accused ... complain of ill-health ... and I think his appearance reveals a state of emaciation. The application should therefore be granted."*

The Amendment of Criminal Procedure Code by N.R.C.D. 309 made express provision for the refusal to grant bail under certain circumstances such as treason, subversion, murder, robbery, hijacking, piracy or escape from unlawful custody or whether a person is being held for extradition to a foreign country. Unlike N.R.C.D. 309, the previous provision in Act 30 only implied that all persons accused of committing murder should be refused bail but did not specify other crimes for refusal of bail out rightly. Even though the N.R.C.D. 309 had been expressed about the crimes under which bail should be refused, the learned judge made an interesting remark by drawing the attention of the Attorney General to the fact that yes, the Decree prevented the court from granting bail to persons accused of committing certain crimes but the Decree did not make any express provision on bail in connection to attempted murder and for that matter, attempt on the crime which were listed in the same Decree.

Consequently, the powers of the court to grant bail in cases of murder treason and subversion were curtailed as reflected in cases such as DOGBE and others v. THE REPUBLIC,[22] where an application for bail was not granted because the accused persons had been charged with murder. However, the court in the case of PRAH and Others v THE REPUBLIC[23] granted an application for bail for accused charged with murder because their application for bail together with supporting affidavit indicated that they have been falsely accused of the crime of murder and that the State Attorney did not object to their bail application. Moreover the court stated that the Decree amending Act 30 appears only to cause injustice and hardship to innocent suspects instead of protecting life, liberty and property.

22 (1976) 2 GLR 82
23 (1976) 2 GLR 278

In SIEDU and Others v THE REPUBLIC,[24] the court held that *"Before the enactment of Act 30, s. 96 as amended by N.R.C.D. 309 the granting of bail in murder cases was not unknown although it was uncommon and no one doubted the power of the High Court to grant bail in such cases...The careful reading of Act 30 s. 96 (7) as amended by N.R.C.D. 309 especially having regard to the phrase "shall refuse" would suggest that the legislature …was saying that the court should not exercise the power in murder cases... The presumption was that the legislature did not intend what was inconvenient or unreasonable. Those whom the legislature intended section 96 … to cover were those against whom, the charge of murder preferred would be said by the court to be supported by evidence which the prosecution professed to have and not persons against whom there was not legally accepted evidence connecting them with the charge of murder..."*

Therefore, bail was granted in the Seidu case because of insufficient evidence to support the charge of murder. The court's decision in Seidu did not depart from the previous opinions taken by other courts as discussed above but sought to give the mischief rule interpretation of the status rather than sticking to the plain dictionary meaning. In OWUSU and Another v THE REPUBLIC[25] the High Court in granting an application for bail by accused persons who had been incarcerated for three years pending trial held that *"section 96 (7)(a) of Act 30 as amended by N.R.C.D. 309 did not say that the court should refuse bail when a person was charged with any of the offences specified, but rather it said that the court should refuse bail in cases of murder, treason, subversion, robbery etc… only when on the summary of evidence a case of murder, treason, subversion, robbery etc could be said to have been committed…The Constitution 1979 Article 21 …. unlike Act 30 section 96(7) did not discriminate against the nature of the offence and the Act was subordinate to it. Parliament would not purport to take away or restrict the power conferred on the court by the Constitution to grant bail when a person arrested, restricted or detained in circumstances as were mentioned in article 21 (3)(b) was not tried within a reasonable time. Three years incarceration without trial was an unreasonable time especially when it was said to affect the health of the applicants..."*

The width of interpretation which has been given seem to get wider by each case that surfaces on the issue of bail. In murder cases the interpretation given by the court and this case is that the provision under N.R.C.D. 309 does not curtail the powers of the court in granting bail. This seems to be a digression

24 (1978) 1 GLR 65
25 (1980) GLR 679

of opinion from the previous decisions in the above named case where there seems to be an acceptance of the fact that the court's powers to grant bail had been curtailed.

However, in a similar case where the trial was delayed for three years, the court in the case of BREFOH v THE REPUBLIC[26] refused to grant bail to the accused because the delay in the opinion of the court was not unreasonable because the delay was neither the fault of the Attorney General nor the court but due to the heavy schedule of the court.

In the case of the REPULIC v. CRENTSIL[27] and Another, the court refused to revoke bail granted to the accused stating that the only basis the court can withdraw the bail granted was when the condition attached had been violated or where the court's decision was illegal or void and not necessarily because the prosecution has discovered new sufficient scientific evidence which either points to the guilt of the accused.

The question of whether bail could be granted when the applicant has been charged with the offence of subversion/ stealing was addressed in the case of BOATENG and Another v THE REPUBLIC.[28] The court held that since the charge of stealing cocoa was included in the definition of the offence of subversion, under the Subversion Decree, 1972 (N.R.C.D. 90), the court was precluded under section 96 (7) (a) of Act 30 as amended by N.R.C.D. 309 from granting the application for bail pending trial. The court simply reiterated the point that the court's power to grant bail had been curtailed except in circumstance, where the applicant's request fell within the ambit of Article 15 of the 1969 Constitution.

Even after the overthrow of the 1969 Constitution, the courts in the matter of OKOE v THE REPUBLIC,[29] granted bail to an accused person, who was arraigned before the circuit court on a charge of forcible entry onto land with violence (trespass). The court in granting the application stated that *notwithstanding the suspension of the 1969 Constitution, Article 15 (3) (b) and (4) of the Constitution was still operative under section 3 (2) of the National Redemption Council Proclamation, 1972 and also governed the grant of bail to accused persons once an accused person was not tried within a reasonable time. The effect was that the accused person, without prejudice to any further proceedings that might be brought against him, was mandatorily entitled to be*

26 (1980) GLR 679
27 (1987-88) 2 GLR 712
28 (1976) 2 GLR 444
29 (1976) 1 GLR p. 80

*released either unconditionally or upon reasonable conditions including such conditions as were reasonable to secure his attendance at the trial.*

However, a different view was taken by the court in the subversion case of DONKOR v. THE REPUBLIC[30] where the accused applied for bail on the grounds that there had been an unreasonable delay in prosecuting his case in terms of Article 15 (3) (b) and (4) of the 1969 Constitution. The court refused the application for bail and held that due to the coup d'état the National Redemption Council (Establishment) Proclamation session 2(1) suspended the 1969 Constitution and the fundamental human right provisions of which Article 15 were not saved and therefore by section 96(7) of Act 30 the court had no power to grant bail.

In the case of MARFO v THE REPUBLIC,[31] the accused, who had been charged with fraud by false pretence contrary to section 132 of the Criminal Code 1960 (Act 29) applied for bail pending trial. In resisting the grant of bail pending trial Counsel for the Republic, submitted that any bail granted by the High Court by virtue of its power under section 96 (2) of the Criminal Procedure Code 1960 (Act 30) would be void and of no legal effect if it was granted without the prior knowledge of the Attorney General. The court granted the application and held that *the proposition that bail granted by the High Court by virtue of its powers under section 96 (2) of Act 30 would be void and of no legal effect if it was granted without the prior knowledge of the Attorney-General was untenable. Consequently, although the practice was prevalent whereby in matters of bail pending trial of criminal offences, the Attorney-General was notified, that practice had never been a statutory essential or mandatory condition to the grant of pre-trial bail. In the instant case, the averments in the affidavit in support of the accused's application disclosed a prima facie case for bail and what was more, an offence involving a meager sum of ¢2,000 was not so serious an offence as to justify a court refusing bail to the offender who was prepared to secure his appearance for trial.*

In addition, the Court also stated that the traditional rule in criminal justice …was that, even where there is an error in the proceeding, the court do not quarrel if the error inures to the benefits of a person accused of a criminal offence. Trouble arises only when the arrow or irregularity inures to deprive the accused of his constitutional rights. Bail is so fundamental that it should not be treated with levity. The above case does not give any view of the

30 (1977) 2 GLR p. 383
31 (1981) GLR p. 722

questions of granting bail before trial but rather recaps the decisions given in the other cases under different crimes.

## Bail Pending An Appeal

As early as the 1960s, the issue of bail pending an appeal was raised in the High Court case of DJABA v. THE REPUBLIC[32]. The applicant, who was convicted in the High Court of the offence of conspiracy to steal and stealing, applied to the High Court for bail pending his appeal to the Supreme Court. The court in granting the application for bail held that "*The conditions governing grant of bail pending appeal should be (i) whether from the record there was a chance of success in the appeal, (ii) whether the appellant would turn up at the hearing and (iii) whether his imprisonment would have worked hardship in the event of the appeal succeeding.*" The decision of the court implies that once the above conditions are met the court would definitely grant an application for bail pending appeal.

However, in 1967 the Court of Appeal in the case of OWUSU and Another v THE STATE,[33] dismissing an application for bail pending appeal held that the granting of bail pending appeal is discretionary and "*(1) that bail would not be granted pending an appeal save in exceptional circumstances or where the hearing of an appeal was likely to be unduly delayed; (2) that in dealing with the latter class of case the court would have regard not only to the length of time which must elapse before the appeal could be heard but also to the length of the sentence to be appealed from, and further that those two matters would be considered in relation to one another; and (3) where the court was satisfied that the conviction was prima facie erroneous either in law or in fact, and that there would be apparent miscarriage of justice if bail was refused.*"

So the issue of whether or not the applicant will turn up during the appeal was not even considered but rather the delay of the appeal proceedings plays a greater role in the granting of bail pending an appeal. The only ground, which seemed to have been maintained, is whether the refusal of bail would work an injustice to the appellant.

After the promulgation of the 1969 Constitution, the court in the case of OKYERE AND ANOTHER v THE REPUBLIC[34] held that prior to the coming

32 (1966) GLR 575 SC
33 (1967) GLR 435 CA
34 (1972) 1 GLR 99

into force of the 1969 Constitution, the basis for granting bail pending an appeal was "*...if there are exceptional or unusual grounds for the applications because the conviction may be prima facie wrong, and the appeal therefore may have obvious prospects of success coupled with the probability that having regard to the shortness of the sentence imposed the hearing of the appeal may be unduly delayed.*" However, after the "*...enactment of the Constitution, 1969, there is an additional ground for granting bail pending appeal, namely, where it is apparent from the judgment or other materials before the court that there is prima facie breach of any of the fundamental rights guaranteed under article 20 of the Constitution during the trial of the accused, the court ought not to refuse the grant of bail.*"

The BEHOME v THE REPUBLIC[35] case seems to be the only case, which has expressly addressed the issue of what happens to persons who have been granted bail pending appeal but are not successful in their appeal. The court's position was that "*There was no general principle of law that once an appellant had been granted bail pending an appeal he could on no account be sent back to prison if his appeal failed. However in the instant case the appellant had, at the time of his release, served a very substantial part of his sentence on the other counts and subject to good behaviour would have had a rebate of sentence.*" The court, nonetheless, stated that where the accused has served a substantial part of his or her term of imprisonment and was of good behavior, there can be a reduction of sentence. Additionally, where "*...the other accused persons had come out of prison... it would be improper to send the appellant back to prison to serve the outstanding terms. The residue of his term would therefore be commuted into a fine.*"

In the REPUBLIC v. REGISTRAR OF HIGH COURT EX PARTE ATTORNEY-GENERAL,[36] the Supreme Court in dismissing an application for bail held that "*The grant of bail was an exercise of a discretionary power and the main consideration was the likelihood of the person concerned failing to appear for the further proceedings. Bail would not be granted pending an appeal save in exceptional cases or where the hearing of an appeal was likely to be unduly delayed or where the court was satisfied that the conviction was prima facie erroneous.*" Therefore, the likelihood of delay as a basis for granting bail pending appeal has replaced the basis of *hardship caused by further imprisonment* as stated by the Supreme Court in the 1966 Djaba case.

35 (1979) GLR 112
36 (1982-83) 1 GLR 407

After the coming into force of the 1992 Constitution of Ghana, the Supreme Court had the opportunity to address the issue of bail pending an appeal in the case of the REPUBLIC v COURT OF APPEAL EX PARTE ATTORNEY GENERAL also known as the Benneh Case.[37] In that case the Supreme Court dismissed an appeal against the Court of Appeal's decision to grant an appeal for bail in a narcotic case and stated that *"...the accused is presumed to be innocent until it is otherwise established. It would therefore be unjust to deprive him of his right to enjoy his freedom in the absence of any law prohibiting the grant of bail to him."*

From the decision of the Benneh case it can be deduced that as long as the accused has not been proven guilty beyond all reasonable doubt the accused is entitled to enjoy his constitutional right to freedom of movement (bail) if the offence of which he is being accused of does not fall within those offences in which bail was statutorily unavailable. The Supreme Court's decision was not also focused on whether the accused person would appear before the court for further proceedings but the Supreme Court was more concerned about the fundamental human rights of the accused person as enshrined in the 1992 Constitution of Ghana and was not hesitant in protecting the rights of the accused person.

In 2004, the Supreme Court had another opportunity to extensively address the issue of bail in the case of THE REPUBLIC v GORMAN and five others.[38] The court held that *"While one might attempt to derive a presumption of grant of bail from the constitutional presumption of innocence, as Wiredu J.S.C.(as he then was) sought to do in the Benneh case (supra), a stronger basis for a presumption of grant of bail under our Constitution might be found in Article 14. Indeed, Art 14(4) embodies a direct duty to grant bail in a specific situation, i.e. when a person is not tried within a reasonable time...We must also consider the cumulative effect of Art. 14(1) and 14(3), which work on the premise that every person is generally entitled to his liberty except in specified cases, and that even where his liberty is so restricted under one or more of those cases, he must be produced before a court within forty-eight hours, or regain his liberty...Any other reading of the Constitution would lead to the untenable conclusion that every accused person has an automatic right to bail under our Constitution. This presumption is, for example, rebutted in cases where a statute specifically disallows bail based on the nature of the offence, such as the situations outlined in s.96 (7) of the Criminal Procedure Code."*

37 (1998-99) SCGLR 559
38 (2003-2004) SCGLR 784

With the democratic dispensation embedded in the 1992 Constitution of Ghana the Supreme Court recognised the constitutional protections of every individual's right to liberty however the Court was quick to add that even though the 1992 Constitution protects the fundamental human rights of the individual and our criminal justice system also presume the innocence of every accused person until proven guilty beyond reasonable doubt the right to bail is not an automatic right but subject to the laws of Ghana of which the Criminal Procedure Code is one. Irrespective of a statutory provision expressly providing for the refusal of bail in certain cases, the 1992 Constitution is quick to add that when there is an unreasonable delay in procedure then the courts in Ghana are empowered to grant bail to the accused person.

In 2016, the landmark case of MARTIN KPEBU (No. 2) v. ATTORNEY GENERAL,[39] the Supreme Court was called upon to address the inconsistencies between section 96(7) of Act 30 as amended and Articles 14, 15 and 19(2)(c) of the 1992 Constitution. Section 96(7) of Act 30 as amended by Section 7 of Act 633 and also as amended by section 41(1)(a) of the Anti-Terrorism Act, 2008 (Act 762) reads: "A court shall refuse to grant bail-

> *(a) in a case of treason, subversion, murder, robbery, hijacking, piracy, rape and defilement or escape from lawful custody , or acts of terrorism;*
> *(b) where a person is being held for extradition to a foreign country."*

The Supreme Court declared that "*Since the Constitution is the fundamental law of the land, to the extent that article 14(3) and (4) mandate bail for all offences while Act 30, s 96(7) excepts the grant of bail in murder cases, etc the latter is deemed to have been repealed by the former by reason of the inconsistency.*" This was the view taken in the 1976 case of Dogbe v. the Republic.

## Conclusion

The examination of constitutional and statutory provisions, as well as case law in Ghana, for the past sixty (60) years of independence, indicate that the fundamental rights of Ghanaians have always been upheld by the courts but the constitutional presumption of innocence does not import an automatic right to bail and that bail is discretionary. However, in the case of police enquiry bail, there is a duty on the police to grant bail after detention of forty-eight hours or take the accused person to the court for any extension of the detention.

The recent decision of the Supreme Court in the Kpedu case, which is in line with the 1970s decisions of the courts in Ghana, requires that as long as the accused or convicted person is not tried within a reasonable time, the courts have the discretion to grant bail irrespective of the nature of accusation or the severity of the punishment upon conviction. This has removed the statutory restriction on the granting of bail in murder, rape, defilement, rape, robbery and other cases.

"For justice while she winks at crime, stumbles on innocent sometimes"[40] and thus there is the need to constantly review the law on bail in Ghana to be dynamic to reflect changing times since so much discretion has been vested in the courts in the granting of bail.

40  Samuel Butler, Hudibras, 1663-1678, as cited in The Quotable Lawyer at p.156

# 5

# PRESIDENTIAL GRANT OF PARDON AND RULE OF LAW: THE CASE OF MONTIE TRIO

## Lydia A. Nkansah
## Maame Efua Addadzi - Koom

**Abstract**

In August 2016, the former President of Ghana, John Dramani Mahama granted pardon to the Montie trio who had been convicted for contempt of court following offending statements against the Chief Justice and other Justices of the Supreme Court of Ghana sitting on a pending case. The pardon remitted the remaining three months of a four-month prison sentence meted out to the contemnors. The grant of the pardon sparked a lot of debate which partly centered on the legality of the President's exercise of his pardon power especially in relation to the offence of contempt of court as provided for in the 1992 Constitution. Other issues raised were whether the Presidential pardon is discretionary and subject to Article 296? And whether it is absolute or are there limitations to it? Does the consultation with the Council of State provide a viable accountability for the presidential exercise of pardon? In this paper we argue that the grant of pardon exercised by the President, although legal was not legitimate. Our argument is based on the premise that in a constitutional democracy, rule of law – the requirement of legality, acting according to law has a higher connotation than the law.

## I. Introduction

### 1.1 Background

In August 2016, the former President of The Republic of Ghana John Dramani Mahama granted pardon[1] to the Montie trio who had been convicted for contempt of court and sentenced with four months imprisonment. They had served for one month out of the four months prison term. The pardon remitted the remaining prison sentence of the contemnors. The remission was effective August 26, 2016.[2]

The Montie trio, Salifu Maase, alias Mugabe, a radio show host; Godwin Ako Gunn and Alistair Tairo Nelson, two political commentators on June 29, 2016, the eve of Martyrs Day commemoration[3], during a radio discussion on a case pending in the Supreme Court against the Electoral Commission[4] made threats to rape the Chief Justice of Ghana, Georgina Theodora Wood and also threatened to "finish" the other Supreme Court judges as well as High

---

1 There are a few differences between 'pardon' and other terminologies such as 'commutation', 'clemency' and 'amnesty'. Clemency (executive clemency) is the umbrella term that constitutes pardon, commutation and amnesty. Pardon usually remits the full the consequences of criminal conviction and may be subject to conditions precedent or subsequent. Commutations is simply partial pardon.Amnesty is a pardon for war-related crimes.: Charles Shanor & Marc Miller, 'Pardon Us: Systematic Presidential Pardons' (2001) 2 <https://dx.doi.org/10.2139/ssrn.26343> accessed 18 November 2016. However, the differences are not essential for the purpose of this paper. 'Pardon' is used in a general sense and carries the import of article 72 of the 1992 Constitution which mirrors the technical meaning of the bigger set clemency. 'Pardon' is used interchangeably with 'Prerogative of mercy' in this paper.

2 Nathan Gadugah, 'Mahama frees Montie 3' (*Myjoyonline*, 22 August 2016) <http://www. myjoyonline.com/politics/2016/August-22nd/mahama-pardons-montie-3.php> accessed 6 January 2017.

3 Martyrs Day is a day set aside to remember three Justices of the High Court of Ghana who were abducted and murdered about 34 years ago on June 30 1982. The three justices were Mr. Justice Fred Poku Sarkodee, Mrs. Justice Cecilia Koranteng-Addow and Mr. Justice Kwadwo Agyei Agyepong.

4 The pending case, *Abu Ramadan & Evans Nimako v. Electoral Commission & Attorney General* Writ No. J1/14/2016, was an action brought by the plaintiffs in the Supreme Court seeking for a declaration and order that the names of voters who registered with the National Health Insurance Scheme (NHIS) cards be removed from the voters' register by the Electoral Commission as the NHIS cards were not valid national identification cards.

Court judges sitting on the case.[5] The trio made these threats on 'Pampaso', a political radio programme on Montie FM in Accra, based on their belief that the judges sitting on the case intended to instigate violence during the 2016 presidential and parliamentary elections. The trio emphatically stated that, they knew the homes of the sitting judges and will "finish" them should there be violence during the 2016 elections. They cautioned the sitting judges to be mindful of their actions lest they suffered the same fate as the High Court judges who were abducted, killed and burnt during the revolution era in Ghana some 34 years ago.[6] Their comments were greeted with disapproval and were condemned by a segment of the Ghanaian citizenry. The trio were hauled before the Supreme Court, charged and convicted with contempt of court. On July 27, 2016 the Supreme Court of Ghana sentenced the trio to four months imprisonment together with a fine of GH¢ 10, 000 each. They were convicted for contempt of court on three grounds of scandalizing the court; defying and lowering the authority of the court; and bringing the name of the court into disrepute.

President Mahama invoked his power under Article 72 of the 1992 Constitution and pardoned the Montie trio in response to two separate petitions presented to the him. One of the petitions was presented by the lawyers of the contemnors and the other petition which was endorsed by party supporters of the sitting government and Ministers of State was presented by the Research and Advocacy Platform (RAP). A communiqué from the Presidency signed by the Communications Minister, indicated that President Mahama granted the pardon based on compassionate grounds.[7] That is, based on the remorse of the trio and their subsequent retraction of their offending comments. In an interview on Metro TV's Good Evening Ghana, President Mahama indicated that serving the extra three months by the montie trio would not have been in anybody's interest.[8] President Mahama in explaining his rationale for exercising the Article 72 pardon power said,

5 Gadugah (n 2). As a result of these threats some of the Judges who names were mentioned during the discussion had to recuse themselves. Chief Justice Georgina Woode and Justice Nasiru Sulemana Gbadegbe who recused themselves and were replaced by Justices Akuffo and Ansah.: Kweku Zurek, 'Chief Justice, Gbadegbe recuse themselves from Montie FM contempt case' (*Graphic Online*, 12 July 2016) <url> accessed 8 January 2017.

6 See on Martyrs Day *supra* (n 3).

7 Gadugah (n 2).

8 Mohammed Ali, 'Monte 3 pardon was in the interest of Ghana - Prez Mahama' (*Graphic Online*, 6 September 2016) <http://www.graphic.com.gh/news/general-news/montie-3-pardon-was-in-the-interest-of-ghana-prez-mahama.html> accessed 6 January 2017.

They remain convicted and that's what a lot of people do not realize. They remain convicted, they paid GH¢ 30, 000 in fines and that money is in the state coffers. But what I did was that, instead of letting them spend four months in prison, they spent one month in prison. Indeed if you look at the conviction and the sentencing, the general consensus was that, four months was quite a harsh punishment to have been imposed for that kind of crime. *And so I believe that I acted constitutionally and it was in the interest of Ghana.*[9]

The President further explained that he did not exercise his power arbitrarily because he acted in consultation with the Council of State as the Constitution, 1992 prescribes.[10]

Prior to grant of pardon, Lawyer Elikplim Agbemava filed a petition for interlocutory injunction in the Supreme Court for the true and proper interpretation of Article 72 and article 296 of the Constitution, 1992. Mr. Agbemava's action was in anticipation of preventing the president from pardoning the Montie trio.[11] Subsequent lawsuits were filed by private citizens after the pardon was granted, all of which are currently pending before the Supreme court.

### 1.2 The Ensuing Debate

The pardon of the Montie trio sparked a lot of debates and arguments across the country. While some applauded the President for a good work done, others expressed their disapproval.

Alfred Woyome, a business man of the infamous judgment debt scandal stated in support of the pardon of the Montie trio that, the Supreme Court "erred bitterly" in proceedings leading to their conviction as well as its ruling. He applauded the use of the presidential pardon to straighten out the judicial tyranny.[12] Similarly, Mr. Johnson Asiedu Nketia, the General Secretary of

---

9 Ibid. (Emphasis added).

10 Ibid.

11 Malik Abass Daabu, 'Lawyer sues A-G over possible pardon of Montie 3' (*Myjoyonline*, 15 August 2016) <http://www.myjoyonline.com/news/2016/august-15th/lawyer-sues-a-g-over-possible-pardon-of-montie-3.php> accessed 8 January 2017.

12 Enoch Darfah Frimpong, 'Supreme Court "erred bitterly" on Montie 3- Woyome' (*Graphic Online*, 2 August 2016) <http://www.graphic.com.gh/news/politics/supreme-court-erred-bitterly-on-montie-3-woyome.html> accessed 6 January 2017.

the National Democratic Congress (NDC) which is the political party of the Mahama administration, described the debate over the Montie trio pardon as needless because the President acted within his constitutional powers.[13]

On the flipside, the public backlash to the pardon was also quick and insistent. Former President Flt. Lieutenant Jerry John Rawlings grossed out his condemnation of the pardon when he said, "How can you glorify foolishness and recklessness with a senseless decision? It absolutely undermines the judiciary".[14] The then opposition party, New Patriotic Party (NPP) also expressed their disappointment in the decision by President Mahama to pardon the Montie trio. They dismissed the pardon as inappropriate and an endorsement of unacceptable behaviour in the Ghanaian society.[15] The NPP called for the judiciary to reverse the pardon granted by the President and also called on all Ghanaians to vote out the Mahama administration come the December 7, 2016 elections.[16]

Martin Amidu, a former Attorney General and Minister of Justice dismissed the jail sentence of the Montie trio as unconstitutional on the grounds of procedural errors and an abuse of the fundamental human rights of the contemnors. This notwithstanding, the former Attorney General expressed his repugnance towards the petition for presidential pardon. He wrote,

> I find the immediate resort by the lawyers for the contemnors to petitioning the President for pardon for the contemnors revolting *having regards to the context of the case, the background of the contemnors and their association with the Government of the day. It embarrasses and encumbers the Presidential power of mercy which he may exercise...*"[17]

13 Delali Adogla, 'Debate over Montie 3 pardon needless - Asiedu Nketia' (*Citifmonline*, 23 August 2016) <http://citifmonline.com/2016/08/23/debate-over-montie-3-pardon-needless-asiedu-nketia/> accessed 6 January 2017.

14 Rawlings: "Montie 3" Pardon is the Most useless and senseless decision a leader can ever make. (*The Statesmanonline* 26 August 2016) <http://thestatesmanonline.com/index.php/politics/2037-rawlings-montie-3-pardon-is-the-most-useless-decision-a-leader-can-ever-make> accessed 6 January 2017.

15 Reverse Montie 3 pardon now- NPP demands (*Ghanaweb* 22 August 2016) <http://mobile.ghanaweb.com/GhanaHomePage/pressreleases/Reverse-Montie-3-pardon-now-NPP-demands-464400> accessed 6 January 2017.

16 Ibid.

17 Jasmine Arku, 'Supreme Court had no power to jail Montie trio-Martin Amidu' (*Graphic Online*, 17 August 2016) <http://www.graphic.com.gh/news/general-news/supreme-court-had-no-power-to-jail-montie-trio-martin-amidu..html> accessed 8 January 2017.

In spite of finding the petition revolting, Martin Amidu acknowledged the legality of the exercise of prerogative of mercy and dismissed the argument that the grant of pardon interfered with the independence of the judiciary. He argued that every exercise of pardon was an interference with judicial independence in the sense that it pardons convictions and/or sentences already imposed in exercise of the Court's judicial power. That is why it is a prerogative of mercy!: to grant to a person convicted of an offence a pardon, he stated.[18] The problem Mr. Amidu identified which shrouded the entire turn of events was the partisan political colour it took and the fact that the event occurred in an election year.[19]

Ace Annan Ankomah, a private legal practitioner indicated that there could be an application for a review of the President's grant of pardon to the Montie trio at the Supreme Court. In light of this direction for a review, there is currently a consolidated case by private citizens before the Supreme Court. One such private citizen is a Sunyani-based legal practitioner, Mr. Alfred Tuah Yeboah who filed a suit against the Attorney-General to reverse the remission of the Montie trio sentences. Lawyer Tuah Yeboah prayed the Supreme Court for a declaration that on a true and proper interpretation of Article 72 of the 1992 Constitution, the president's power of prerogative of mercy "is limited to convictions 'for criminal offences' and does not include convictions for contempt arising from the inherent jurisdiction of the court…". Lawyer Tuah Yeboah was thus, questioning the legality of the President's grant of pardon remitting the jail sentence of the Montie trio.[20]

The ensuing debates partly centered on the legality of the President's exercise of his pardon power especially in relation to the offence of contempt of court as provided for in the 1992 Constitution. Other issues raised were whether the Presidential pardon is discretionary and subject to Article 296? And whether it is absolute or are there limitations to it? Does the consultation with the Council of State provide a viable accountability for the presidential exercise of pardon?

In this paper we argue that the grant of pardon exercised by the President, although legal was not legitimate. The pardon power was duly exercised as far as the constitutionality and legality of the grant of pardon by President Mahama under Article 72 of the 1992 Constitution is concerned. However,

18 Ibid.

19 Ibid.

20 'Lawyer sues A-G; seeks to reverse remission of sentences of Montie 3' (*Myjoyonline*, 29 August 2016) <http://www.myjoyonline.com/news/2016/August-29th-lawyer-sues-a-g-seeks-to-reverse-remission-of-sentences-of-montie-3.php> accessed 6 January 2017.

the legality of the exercise of such power, did not guarantee and uphold legitimacy.

Our argument is based on the premise that in a constitutional democracy, rule of law-the requirement of legality, acting according to law has a higher connotation than the law.[21] Thus, the exercise of legality should result in upholding the higher law. That is the sense of rightness of a given morality.[22] This paper stresses on the legality-legitimacy dichotomy within the context of the exercise of presidential pardon. Our claim is that, President Mahama's grant of pardon was legal but his grant of pardon lacked legitimacy considering factors such as the interest of Ghanaians, the manner in which the President exercised his discretion and the fact that the offence for which they had been convicted was in defiance of judicial authority.

This paper is structured to flesh out our argument as follows: part two focuses on discussing the intricacies of the concept of pardon; part three is on the law on the grant of pardon in Ghana; part four reviews the pardon granted by the President while the final part suggests the way forward regarding the exercise of presidential pardon, particularly the limits within which such power should be exercised and the possibility of using the pardon power as a tool for systematic policy.

## II. The Concept of Pardon

### 2.1 Historical Background and the UK Perspective on Pardon

Pardon is an official act of grace that is bestowed on a person or persons to free them from their punishment either partially or wholly. The English royal prerogative of mercy served as an ancillary feature that was instituted to reduce the harshness of common law crimes. Pardon was an English monarchical power, a broad royal fiat. This power existed long before the Norman invasion.[23] History shows that the pardon power was not primarily for mercy as is the case today. The royal fiat was for raising funds and armies. That is, the beneficiaries of pardon, were pardoned on condition that they

21 Hilaire Barnett, *Constitutional and Administrative Law* (4th edn, Cavendish Publishing Ltd. 2002)

22 Ibid.

23 Brian C. Kalt, 'Pardon Me?: The Constitutional Case Against Presidential Self -Pardons' (1996) 106 Yale LJ 782 <https://papers.ssrn.com/sol3/papers.cfm?abstract_id=1312000> accessed 18 November 2016.

24 Ibid.

make some cash payment or made a promise to join the military.[24] However, with the passage of time, the scope of the royal pardon expanded and became absolute in respect only of offences against the state.[25]

At present the exercise of the prerogative of mercy in the U.K. is by the Constitutional Monarch who acts on the advice of the Home Secretary.[26] It is no longer the prerogative of the sovereign and it is subject to judicial review within a limited scope.[27] The decision of the Home Secretary is also amenable to judicial review in some cases.[28] In *R v. Secretary of State for the Home Department; Ex parte Bentley*[29] the Court held that the formulation of policy for the grant of a free pardon was not justiciable but a failure to recognize that the prerogative of mercy was capable of being exercised in many different circumstances and over a wide range. It was held that the prerogative power of mercy may be reviewed on the grounds similar to those on which the exercise of statutory powers is reviewed, namely for illegality, irrationality and procedural impropriety.

Pardon is primarily individualized and mercy-driven.[30] Each case is to be treated individually based on its facts.[31] Many legal systems including Ghana have codified this power in their Constitution.[32]

## 2.2 The American Jurisprudence on Pardon

Article II, § 2, cl. 1 of the U.S. Constitution provides that "The president shall…have Power to grant Reprives and Pardons for Offenses against the

---

25 Ibid.

26 Pardoning Power in the UK, USA and Canada: A Comparative Analysis. Chapter V 213-252 available at Shodhganga <http://shodhganga.inflibnet.ac.in/bitstream/10603/148889/12/12_chapter%205.pdf> accessed July 12 2017.

27 Ibid.

28 Pardoning Power in the UK, USA and Canada: A Comparative Analysis. Chapter V 213-252 available at Shodhganga <http://shodhganga.inflibnet.ac.in/bitstream/10603/148889/12/12_chapter%205.pdf> accessed July 12 2017.

29 (1994) QB 349.

30 Shanor & Miller (n 1) at 2.

31 See Schick v. Reed 419 U.S. 256, 265 (1974).

32 For example, sections 175 and 212 of the 1999 Constitution of the Federal Republic of Nigeria (as amended) provides for prerogative of mercy. Section 121 of the 1995 Constitution of the Republic of Uganda also addresses prerogative of mercy. The Pakistan Constitution of 1973 also provides for granting of pardon under article 45 while the 1972 Bangladesh Constitution does same under article 49.

33 32 U.S. (7 Pet.) 150 (1833).

United States, except in Cases of Impeachment." In *United States v. Wilson*[33] the Supreme Court per Chief Justice Marshall defined pardon to be 'an act of grace, proceeding from the power entrusted with the execution of the laws, which exempts the individual, on whom it is bestowed, from the punishment the law inflicts for a crime he committed'[34]. The pardon power under the U.S. Constitution has been described as a plenary authority.[35] That is an absolute and unrestricted authority.

The Supreme Court of the United States has construed the pardon power under this provision to be exclusive and unlimited.[36] The Klein court held that "to the executive alone is entrusted the power of pardon, and it is granted without limit."[37] The president exercises his pardon power in cases of violation of federal law on the advice of the Office of Pardon Attorney.

The grant of pardon is justified on moral grounds in *Ex parte Wells*[38], as necessary to avoid a deficiency in the political morality of government. The plenary nature of pardon in the United States is the reason for which there are no laid down standards to guide the exercise of such power. Thus in the U.S. there are very few cases on the appropriateness of the use of pardon power to pardon particular individuals[39] although there have been concerns on the abuse of the pardon power in academia. Paul Larkin Jr. in an article described the president abuse of pardon as having poisoned the well. To buttress his assertion, Larkin Jr. cited the example of clemency recipients under President Bill Clinton's administration who were often people (or their representatives) with strong White House connections or who had contributed generously to the president's party or his own presidential library.[40] To him, Clinton's

34 Ibid at 160.

35 Schick v. Reed (n 31). See Kalt (n 23). See also Samuel T. Morison, 'The Politics of Grace: On the Moral Justification of Executive Clemency' Buffalo Criminal Law Review Vol 9 (2005) 101 - 237 accessed 18 November 2016

36 Ex parte Garland 71 U.S. (4 Wall) 333, 380 (1866).

37 United States v. Klein 80 U.S. (13 Wall. 128, 147 (1871).

38 59 U.S. (18 How.) 307, 310 (1856)

39 William M. Landes & Richard A. Posner, 'The Economics of Presidential Pardons and Commutations' (2007) John M. Olin Law & Economics Working Paper N. 320 (2D SERIES), <http://ssrn.com/abstract_id=956190> accessed 18 November 2016. See also Paul Larkin Jr., 'Revitalizing the Clemency Process' Harvard Journal of Law & Public Policy.

40 Larkin *supra* (n 39).

41 Ibid.

clemency decisions have left a pall over the entire process.[41]

In spite of the plenary nature of the pardon power under the U.S. Constitution, the underlying rationale for the power is clear. Justice Holmes in the American case of *Biddle v. Perovich*[42] aptly stated the rationale for the grant of pardon:

> A pardon in our days is not a private act of grace from an individual happening to possess power. It is a part of the constitutional scheme. When granted, it is the determination of the ultimate authority that the public welfare will be better served by inflicting less than what the judgment fixed.

Chief Justice Burger also enunciated the purpose of pardon power in *Schick v. Reed*[43] thus, 'the plain purpose of the broad power conferred…was to allow plenary authority in the President to "forgive" the convicted person in part or entirely, to reduce a penalty in terms of a specific number of years or to alter it with conditions which are themselves constitutionally unobjectionable.'[44]

The American jurisprudence on pardon therefore reveals that pardon power is plenary, absolute and unrestricted, subject only to the limitations of the wording of the Constitution.

## 2.3 The Indian Jurisprudence on Pardon

The Indian Constitution of 1949 grants unfettered powers of pardon to the President under Article 72. The article provides:

> (1) The President shall have the power to grant pardons, reprieves, respites or remissions of punishment or to suspend, remit or commute the sentence of any person convicted of any offence—
>> (a) in all cases where the punishment or sentence is by a Court Martial;
>> (b) in all cases where the punishment or sentence is for an offence against any law relating to a matter to which the executive power of the Union extends;

42 274 U.S. 480 (1927).
43 419 U.S. 256, at 266 (1974)
44 Ibid.

(c) in all cases where the sentence is a sentence of death.

(2) Nothing in sub-clause (a) of clause (1) shall affect the power conferred by law on any officer of the Armed Forces of the Union to suspend, remit or commute a sentence passed by a Court Martial.

(3) Nothing in sub-clause (c) of clause (1) shall affect the power to suspend, remit or commute a sentence of death exercisable by the Governor of a State under any law for the time being in force.[45]

Governors of States are also conferred with pardon power under Article 161 of the Indian Constitution of 1949. However, the pardon power of the President is wider than that of the Governors of States. The President's pardon power extends to punishments or sentences by a Court martial as well as death sentences but the power of pardon of Governors of State does not. The process of granting pardon in India is initiated by filing a petition under Article 72 of the Indian Constitution, 1949.

The President exercises his pardon power on the advice of the Council of Ministers. In *Maru Ram v. Union of India*[46] the Constitutional Bench of the Supreme Court of India held that the exercise of the pardon power by the President is not to be exercised independent of the advice of the Central Government. This advice binds the Head of State.[47] The President's exercise of pardon power is *prima facie* not justiciable because of its exclusive administrative nature. However, the *Maru Ram* court held that where the pardon power was exercised mala fide or arbitrarily, then the exercise of the pardon could be subject to judicial review. The court stated:

> *Pardon, using this expression in the amplest connotation, ordains fair exercise, as we have indicated above. Political vendetta or party favoritism cannot be interlopers in this area. The order which is the product of extraneous or mala fide factors will vitiate the exercise* …For example, if the Chief Minister of State releases everyone in the prisons in his State on his birthday or because a son has been born to him, it will be an outrage on the Constitution to let such madness survive.[48]

45 Indian Constitution 1949.

46 1981 (1) SCC 017

47 This was reiterated by the Indian Supreme Court in *Dhananjoy Chatterjee alias Dhana v. State of West Bengal* (1994) 2 SCC 220.

48 Ibid (emphasis added).

The Indian Supreme Court again in *Kehar Singh v. Union of India*[49] recognized the need for pardon to correct the fallibility of human judgment and further held that pardon cannot be claimed as a matter of right. It also stated that "the question as to the area of the President's power under Article 72 falls squarely within the judicial domain and can be examined by the court by way of judicial review. However, the order of the President cannot be subjected to judicial review on its merits except within the strict limitations defined in *Maru Ram v. Union of India...*". The facts leading to the decision in *Kehar Singh v. Union of India* are as follows: Kehar Singh had been convicted of murder and conspiracy for the assasination of the then Prime Minister of India and had been given a death sentence. Singh's son appealed but his appeal was dismissed. Singh's son therefore petitioned the President to grant pardon to his father. However, the president rejected his petition.

The principle on whether pardon power was subject to judicial review was settled in the landmark case of *Epuru Sudhakar & Another v. Government of Andhra Pradesh & Others.*[50] The court held that there is a limited judicial review of the exercise of pardon power on grounds which were enumerated by Pasayat, J. as follows: (a) That the order has been passed without application of mind; (b) That the order is mala fide; (c) That the order has been passed on extraneous or wholly irrelevant considerations; (d) That the order suffers from arbitrariness.[51]

It is settled law in India that pardon power under both Articles 72 and 161 of the Indian Constitution, 1949 is subject to judicial scrutiny.[52]

## 2.4 Grant of Pardon in Kenya

Under the repealed Constitution of Kenya, 1963 the President was bestowed with a prerogative of mercy under section 27. Section 28 established an Advisory Committee on Prerogative of Mercy whose members were appointed by the President. The President was however, not bound to comply with the

49 AIR 1989 SC 653.

50 (2006) 8 SCC 161.

51 Although this case was decided on facts pertaining to the exercise of pardon power by a Governor of State rather than the President, the principles still applies. See Suresh V. Nadagoudar and SanjeeveGowda.G.S, 'Presidential Power to Pardon in India: An Overview' *International Journal of Law and Legal Jurisprudence Studies.*

52 Abhimanyu Kumar, Pardoning Power under the Indian Constitution (2009) <http://ssrn.com/abstract=1427237> accessed July 12 2017. See also Nadagoudar (n 51).

advice of the Committee.[53] Section 29 of the 1963 Kenyan Constitution titled "Functions of Advisory Committee on Prerogative of Mercy"provided that:

(1) Where a person has been sentenced to death (otherwise than by a court-martial) for an offence, the President shall cause a written report of the case from the trial judge, together with such other information derived from the record of the case or elsewhere as *he may require, to be considered at a meeting of the Advisory Committee on the Prerogative of Mercy; and after obtaining the advice of the Committee he shall decide in his own judgment whether to exercise any of his functions under section 27.*

(2) The President may consult with the Committee before deciding whether to exercise any of his functions under section 27 in a case not falling within subsection (1), but *he shall not be obliged to act in accordance with the advice of the Committee.*

Under this boundless regime, the President abused his pardon power and was criticized by the media and other human rights organizations.[54] Particularly striking is the pardon of Dr. Margaret Gachara, the head of the National Aids Control Council (NAAC) in 2004. Margaret Gachara was convicted of abuse of office and obtaining KES 27 million by false pretences and sentenced to 12 months imprisonment on three counts which were to run concurrently in August, 2004.[55] However, she was granted pardon in December of the same year. The short sentence and speedy pardon attracted criticisms.[56]

The Gachara scandal among other examples of abuse of pardon power influenced the drafting of the new Kenyan Constitution, 2010, which now insists that the President consults the Advisory Committee.[57] The Constitution also provides for an enactment that will detail the processes of the Committee[58] and also gives room for the Committee to consider the views of the victims of the offence committed by the pardonee in making its recommendations to the President.[59] Thus, the express provisions under section 29 of the repealed 1963 Constitution do not appear in the 2010 Kenyan Constitution.

---

53 Section 29 of the Constitution of the Republic of Kenya 1963. See also P.K. Mbote & M. Akech, *Kenya: Justice Sector and the Rule of Law* (African Minds 2011) 68.
54 Mbote & Akech (n 53) supra.
55 Ibid.
56 Ibid.
57 Article 133(1) of Kenyan Constitution, 2010.
58 Article 133(3)
59 Article 133(4).

## 2.5 Conclusion

This part has offered discussion on grant of pardon as it pertains in UK, the United States, India and Kenya.

## III. The Law on Pardon in Ghana

### 3.1 Constitutional Provisions on Pardon

Article 72 of the Constitution, 1992 is the principal provision regulating the grant of pardon in Ghana. Titled, "Prerogative of Mercy" the Article provides:

> (1) *The President may, acting in consultation with the Council of State-*
> (a) *grant to a person convicted of an offence a pardon* either free or subject to lawful conditions; or
> (b) grant to a person a respite, either indefinite or for a specified period, from the execution of punishment imposed on him for an offence; or
> (c) substitute a less severe form of punishment for a punishment imposed on a person for an offence; or
> (d) remit the whole or part of a punishment imposed on a person or of a penalty or forfeiture otherwise due to Government on account on any offence.
> (2) Where a person is sentenced to death for an offence, a written report of the case from the trial judge or judges, together with such other information derived from the record of the case or elsewhere as may be necessary, shall be submitted to the President.
> (3) For the avoidance of doubt, it is hereby declared that a reference in this article to a conviction or the imposition of a punishment, penalty, sentence or forfeiture includes a conviction or the imposition of a punishment, penalty, sentence or forfeiture by a court-marital or other military tribunal.[60]

It is apparent from Article 72 that prerogative of mercy in Ghana is synonymous with the broader clemency umbrella.[61] Article 72 presents a

---

60 1992 Constitution (emphasis added).
61 On clemency, see footnote 1.

constitutional obligation to be merciful. Nonetheless, this legal obligation of mercy is not beyond the effective reach of legitimacy as if the legality and legitimacy were mutually exclusive components of the law.

It is important to point out that the president's prerogative of mercy under the 1992 Constitution is a discretionary power and as such is subject to Article 296 of the Constitution. Article 296 of the 1992 Constitution is a cross-cutting provision that limits the exercise of discretionary powers granted to any person or authority by the Constitution or any other law. It provides:

> Where in this Constitution or in any other law discretionary power is vested in any person or authority -
>
> (a) that discretionary power shall be deemed to imply a duty to be fair and candid;
>
> (b) *the exercise of the discretionary power shall not be arbitrary, capricious or biased wither by resentment, prejudice or personal dislike and shall be in accordance with due process of law;* and
>
> (c) where the person or authority is not a judge or other judicial officer, there shall be published by constitutional instrument or statutory instrument, regulations that are not inconsistent with the provisions of this Constitution or that other law to govern the exercise of the discretionary power.[62]

It goes therefore to say that, Article 296 provides a legitimacy framework of some sort within which legally valid and constitutionally valid powers for that matter should be exercised that is, precluding arbitrariness, capriciousness, bias or prejudice.

### 3.2 In Consultation with the Council of State

Article 72 of the Constitution, 1992 specifically directs that the exercise of the President's pardon should be "in consultation with the the Council of State...". President Mahama duly acknowledged this requirement in an interview on Metro TV's Good Evening Ghana when he explained,

> It [the pardon] must not be arbitrary; and that's why there again; they say it must be in consultation with the Council of State. The

---

62 Emphasis added.

> Council of State is an elderly body; it's a body above the President; some of the members are elected; others have served in very important positions in their lives and so it says the President must consult the council. And so even though they give the President that power, again they put a check on it so that it's not done with arbitrary discretion.[63]

Chapter nine of the Constitution 1992 is on the Council of State. The Constitution provides for the composition of the Council of State under article 89(2). Apart from advising the President in the exercise of pardon, the Council of State also advises the President or any other authority in respect of any appointment which is required by the Constitution or any other law to be made in accordance with the advice of, or in consultation with the Council of State.[64] The Council of State also performs other functions assigned by the Constitution, 1992 and any other law not inconsistent with the Constitution.[65]

In the recent case of *Richard Dela Sky v. Attorney-General (2016)* the Supreme Court on the effect of the recommendation of the Council of State in the appointment of the Chairman of the Electoral Commission by the President under Article 70(2) held that a combined reading of Article 70(2) and article 91(3) of the 1992 Constitution was to the effect that the recommendation of the Council of State was not binding on the President. Article 70(2) which was in contention in this case provides, "The President shall, acting on the advice of the Council of State, appoint the Chairman, Deputy Chairman, and other members of the Electoral Commission". Article 91(3) also provides that, "[t]he Council of State may, upon request or on its own initiative, consider and make recommendations on any matter being considered or dealt with by the President, a Minister of State, Parliament or any other authority established by this Constitution *except that the President, Minister of State, Parliament or other authority shall not be required to act in accordance with any recommendation made by the Council of State under this clause*." The law per the Supreme Court decision in *Richard Dela Sky* case therefore is that, the advice of the Council of State does not bind the president.

From the foregoing, it can be observed first that, Article 72 requires the pardon power to be exercised in consultation with the Council of State and

---

63 Ali, (n 8) *supra*.
64 Article 91(1) of 1992 Constitution of the Republic of Ghana.
65 Article 91(4) of 1992 Constitution of the Republic of Ghana.

secondly, the former President acknowledged this requirement as a check on the exercise of his pardon power. However, by the Supreme Court decision in the *Richard Delay Sky* case, the recommendation of the Council of State as a check on the exercise of pardon power which the former President held on so dearly in his defence falls apart. After all, the Council's decision is not binding on him.

### 3.3 The Practice of the Grant of Pardon

The grant of pardon especially under the fourth republic of Ghana has taken the nature of mass grant usually during festive seasons such as Christmas or New Year or on public holidays. For example, former President Rawlings, before leaving office granted pardon to some 34 prisoners.[66] Under the Kufuor Administration, 130 prisoners were pardoned in 2005 during Ghana's 48th anniversary celebrations.[67] 1,206 prisoners were freed or had their sentences commuted to mark the Ghana at 50 celebrations in 2007.[68] In 2008, another 1410 prisoner were pardoned to mark Republic Day.[69] In January 2009 before the Kufuor Administration handed over, about 500 prisoners were also pardon one of whom was Tsatsu Tsikata.[70] The late President Atta Mills also granted pardon to 1021 prisoners to mark the centenary birthday of Osagyefo Dr. Nkrumah.[71] To commemorate Republic Day, 1st July, President Mahama granted pardon to about 900 prisoners in 2016.[72]

---

66 '34 Pardoned Prisoners Still in Jail' (*Ghanaweb* 21 June 2001) <http://mobile.ghanaweb.com/GhanaHomePage/NewsArchive/34-Pardoned-Prisoners-Still-in-Jail-16120?channel=D1>accessed 6 July 2017.

67 Godwin Yaw Agboka, 'Kufuor's Exercise of the Prerogative of Mercy' (*Ghanaweb* May 27, 2008) <<http://mobile.ghanaweb.com/GhanaHomePage/features/Kufuor-s-exercise-of-the-Prerogative-of-Mercy-144380> accessed 6 July 2017.

68 Ibid.

69 President Kufuor Pardons 1410 Prisoners (*Ghanaweb* Seo 4, 2008) <http://mobile.ghanaweb.com/GhanaHomePage/NewsArchive/President-Kufuor-pardons-1410-prisoners-149561> accessed 6 July 2017.

70 Kufuor Pardons Tsatsu, Kwame Peprah, 500 Others (*Ghanaweb* Jan 7, 2009) <http://mobile.ghanaweb.com/GhanaHomePage/NewsArchive/Kufuor-pardons-Tsatsu-Kwame-Peprah-500-others-155822> accessed July 13 2017.

71 '1021 Prisoners released on pardon', Daily Graphic, September 24, 2009.

72 900 Prisoners Get Presidential Pardon. (*Myjoyonline* June 30, 2015) <http://www.myjoyonline.com/news/2015/June-30th-/900-prisoners-get-presidential-pardon.php>accessed 6 July 2017.

## IV. The Pardon Granted by the President in Montie Trio Saga in Review

This part reviews the pardon power as exercised by President Mahama in the Montie Trio saga. In making our argument that the grant of pardon regarding the Montie trio was in bad taste we review the pardon granted under four main headings namely: grant of pardon for contempt of court, legitimacy, judicious exercise of discretion and defiance of court authority.

### 4.1 The Grant of Pardon and Contempt of Court

The grant of pardon by President Mahama in the Montie trio case was with respect to contempt of court as provided for under article 19(12) of the Constitution, 1992 which states that, "Clause (11) of this article shall not prevent a Superior Court from punishing a person for contempt of itself notwithstanding that the act or omission constituting the contempt is not defined in a written law and the penalty is not so prescribed." Article 19(12) is a replication of the law of contempt which harks back to the English rule which gained authoritative status in *R v. Almon*[73]. Wilmot J observed in that case that, contempt of court is conduct which scandalizes the court and impedes the due administration of justice.[74] Contempt may be *contempt in facie curiae* (contempt in the face of the court) or *ex facie curiae* (contempt committed outside the court).

In the Montie Trio case, the contempt *ex facie* for which they were convicted was not defined in a written law and the penalty for it was not prescribed. Based on this fact, some argue that, the President did not have power to grant pardon in respect of Article 19(12) contempt of court due to the fact that the prerogative of mercy under Article 72 of the Constitution, 1992 does not extend to crimes not written in a law. We do not subscribe to this line of reasoning because the language of Article 72 does not give any indication as to such inferred restriction on the categories of offences which can and cannot be pardoned. Article 19(12) should be interpreted according to the wording of its own limitations and not the limitations which that wording does not import. Article 72 explicitly states that the President may "grant to a person convicted of *an offence* a pardon" and may also "remit the whole or part of a punishment imposed on a person or of a penalty or forfeiture otherwise due

73 (1765) Wilm 243, 255
74 Ibid.

to Government on account *on any offence*." An offence is an offence: written or not; criminal or quasi-criminal. Thus, it is our submission that the President may grant pardon in respect of contempt of court under article 19(12).

A unique feature about the role of the court with regards to conviction for contempt of court in the American Jurisprudence was stated thus,

> Contempt is, of course, a public offence, but it is a special kind of public offence. It is like any infraction of law, an offence against the whole people, but in addition and more important, it is an offence against the dignity and a defiance of the authority of the court. With the conviction of and sentence for an ordinary crime the function of the court ceases; *upon conviction of contempt the court has a direct and vital interest in the enforcement of the penalty*"[75]

Contempt of court under Article 19(12) is therefore a special kind of constitutionally created offence that directly offends the dignity of the court. One which the court has direct interest in the enforcement of its penalty. One which cannot be trifled respecting the grant of pardon.

## 4.2 Legitimacy

According to Hilaire Barnett an English Constitutional Expert, "the rule of law – in its many guises – represents a challenge to state authority and power, demanding that powers both be granted *legitimately and that their exercise is according to law*".[76] In the words of Barnett "according to law means both according to legal rules and something over and above purely formal legality and imputes the concepts of legitimacy and constitutionality. In its turn, legitimacy implies rightness or morality of law".[77] To Hilaire, " the law is not autonomous but rests on the support of those it governs. The law is the servant of the sense of rightness in the community, and whilst the rule of law places the law above every individual-irrespective of rank and station-it remains, paradoxically, subject to the ultimate judgment of the people."[78]

75 Wilbur Larremore, *Constitutional Regulation of Contempt of Court*, Harvard law Review, Vol 13 No. 8 (April 1900), pp. 615--626 at p.622.
76 Barnett (n 21) at 103. (Emphasis added).
77 Ibid.
78 Ibid.

Thus, the rule of law cannot be divorced from legitimacy since it connotes something over and above legality. Legitimacy, like the rule of law, is value laden. As a constitutional democracy, the rule of law is a core value that underlies the entire Constitution of Ghana, 1992. The preamble of the 1992 Constitution expressly declares our commitment to the rule of law as a country. This implies that, legitimacy is ingrained in our core values as country.

The concept of legitimacy has been further categorized into three sub-concepts by Fallon Jr., an American Constitutional law expert. Fallon Jr. measures legitimacy against three objects namely legal, sociological and moral.[79] Legal legitimacy is based on legal norms such that what is lawful is regarded as legitimate. For purposes of this paper, what Fallon Jr. refers to as legal legitimacy has been simply referred to as legality. Legitimacy as a sociological concept is where the public regards an action by a government institution or any official government decision as "justified, appropriate, or otherwise deserving of support for reasons beyond fear of sanctions or mere hope of personal reward".[80] Sociological legitimacy is therefore a variable rather than a constant.[81] Moral legitimacy on the other hand is where legitimacy is accorded moral justifiability or respect-worthiness. Thus, an action or decision of government which is legally correct may not be legitimately correct if it is not justified morally under a moral concept.[82] It is observed that Fallon's sociological and moral legitimacy is what has been labeled as legitimacy simpliciter by Hilaire Barnett. Moving forward, any reference to legality connotes what could otherwise be called legal legitimacy by Fallon Jr. and the use of legitimacy encompasses legitimacy as a sociological and moral concept - what Hilaire Barnnet refers to as the "rightness or morality of law".

As has been started earlier, the Constitution, 1992 bestows on the President the exclusive power to grant pardon under article 72. Thus, the legality of President Mahama's exercise of his prerogative of mercy in favour of the Montie trio, legally speaking is not questionable. As the President himself disclosed, he "acted constitutionally".[83] "Acting constitutionally" literally means he acted "according to law". Considering the President's assertion through the lens of rule of law, the question that needs to be answered is: did the President really

79 Richard H. Fallon Jr. 'Legitimacy and the Constitution' Harvard Law Review Vol 118: 1787 at 1794 (2005) <http://www.jstor.org/stable/4093285 .> accessed 18 November 2016.
80 Ibid at 1795
81 Ibid.
82 Ibid
83 Ali, (n 8) *supra*.

act "according to law", bearing in mind the totality of what "according to law" connotes?

The President acted according to the legal rules laid down under article 72 of the 1992 Constitution but where in the exercise of a legal power the President acts egregiously such as to amount to an abuse of power and discretion, then that act is no longer legitimate.[84] It was against this background that former U.S. President Thomas Jefferson after pushing the Louisiana Purchase[85] through although it was not authorized by the U.S. Constitution wrote, "strict observance of written laws is doubtless one of the high duties of a good citizen, but it is not the highest, for laws of necessity, of self-preservation, of saving our country when in danger are of higher obligation."[86] The converse is true - that when even when the Constitution authorizes an act, reliance on the written law is not conclusive as there is a higher law over and above the written law - the laws of necessity; of self-preservation of our judiciary and core values such as rule of law; and of saving our country when in danger of a higher obligation such as the interest of Ghanaians.

Practice has shown that the moral backdrop of the pardon power is for public welfare that is, in the interest of public. Therefore, it will be illegitimate to follow the law (exercise a constitutionally valid power) when it is not in the interest of the public. President Mahama stated that his exercise of pardon power "was in the interest of Ghana"[87] however all the evidence points in a different direction. Right after the Supreme Court sentenced the contemnors, party faithfuls rallied a pardon the montie trio campaign. By this campaign, a petition book was opened for all supporters of the campaign to sign as a way of piling up pressure on the former President to grant the trio pardon. The speedy pardon which truncated an already short sentence could hardly be in the interest of Ghana. It is crystal clear that the President was coerced into granting the pardon to the Montie trio. His exercise of pardon ceased to be his own decision and by his discretion.

The legality of the pardon power, however strong, is subject to legitimate imperatives. The guiding question in legitimacy is: when is it legitimate to disobey the law or illegitimate to follow the law?[88] The apparent political

84 Fallon Jr, (n 79) at 1843.
85 The Louisiana Purchase was the acquisition of Louisiana territory from France by the United States in 1803.
86 Fallon Jr, (n 79) at 1843.
87 Ali, (n 8) *supra*.
88 Ibid.

party bias which outweighed the interest of Ghanaians made the exercise of President Mahama's pardon power illegitimate. This is one of situations where it was illegitimate to follow the law.

## 4.3 Judicious Exercise of Discretion

Article 296 of the 1992 Constitution regulates the exercise of discretionary power which the Constitution vests in any person or authority. By article 296 such exercise of discretion implies a duty to be fair and candid and a duty not to be arbitrary, capricious or biased whether by resentment, prejudice or personal dislike and shall be in accordance with due process of law. This is the standard against which an abuse of discretionary power may be measured.

We submit that the President's grant of pardon to the Montie trio was a prejudiced politics of grace and biased towards the contemnors who were party faithfuls. His discretion to grant pardon took the colour of politics. The pardon power as exercised by President Mahama drained the power of its ancillary role in correcting injustices and its legitimate force and in its place filled it with political juices. How is it legitimate that the President, is able to use such noble instrument to venture into the justice system of a democratic society and pull out his party faithfuls when they were to serve a rather short term of imprisonment? How is such use of the pardon power in the interest of Ghana when the public outcry says otherwise? President Mahama erred in using the prerogative of mercy in the way he did - it was the first of its kind in the history of the nation. The *Maru Ram* court's rejection of the influence of political vendetta especially in the exercise of pardon power by the president is of persuasive value.

Lastly, in explaining his grant of pardon, President Mahama said that, four months was quite a harsh punishment to have been imposed for that kind of crime.[89] The crime? Contempt of the apex court of Ghana. Is four months harsh enough? In the Gachara case in Kenya, pardon after approximately four months in prison out of a 12 months sentence was considered an improper use of power which stirred up disapproval nationally and internationally.[90] How then is pardon after one month in prison out of four months not an abuse of discretionary power?

89 Ali, (n 8) *supra.*
90 See part 2.4 supra.

## 4.4 Defiance of Court Authority

We indicated earlier that the 1992 Constitution of Ghana is premised among other constitutional principles, on the rule of law espoused in the preamble: "We the people of Ghana, in exercise of our natural and inalienable rights to establish a framework of government…and in solemn declaration and affirmation of our commitment to …**The Rule of Law**;…"[91] The rule of law which connotes both legality and legitimacy cannot be viewed in isolation from political society.[92] Barnett states that, "it is only meaningful to speak of the rule of law in a society which exhibits the features of a democratically elected, responsible – and responsive – government and a separation of powers, which will result in a judiciary which is independent of government."[93] The rule of law in essence ensures that justice prevails in every democratic society.

In the Ghanaian democratic society, the judiciary has been assigned as the administrator of justice under Article 125(1) of the 1992 Constitution. For this reason, the judiciary has been made independent and subject only to the Constitution. It is in view of judicial independence that the Constitution empowers the judiciary under Article 19(12) to convict persons for contempt of itself. The Constitution grants Superior Courts a contempt jurisdiction to preserve the sanctity and dignity of the courts and its administration of justice.[94] The Superior courts being the Supreme Court (which is the apex of all courts in Ghana), the Court of Appeal and the High Court.[95]

In the light of the rationale and foundational principle on which the courts are given inherent jurisdiction to commit for contempt to themselves, it is our argument that President Mahama should not have granted pardon to the Montie trio as it was in defiance of judicial authority.

First of all, the comments by the contemnors was an attack on the respect and confidence of the public in the judiciary and most importantly the highest court in Ghana and its officials including the Chief Justice. Their comments shook the very foundation of dignity and confidence of the general public in the Supreme court and its proceedings. It threatened to weaken the very fabric that firmly the clothed the judiciary with authority and respect. It was

91 Emphasis added.
92 Barnett (n 21 ) at 74.
93 Barnett (n 21) at 73-74.
94 Article 126(2) of the 1992 Constitution.
95 Article 126(1)(a) of 1992 Constitution.

disruptive of the smooth running of the judicial proceedings on the pending case and maligned the administration of justice, so much so that the Chief Justice and another Supreme Court Justice had to recuse themselves.

Also, granting pardon for such contemptuous comments stood the risk of eroding the highly placed role of the judiciary as custodians of justice. Their comments led to fear-mongering among judicial officers especially because of the historical backdrop and timing of their utterance. As a country our past reminds us of a gory event where three High court judges were abducted and murdered. By a curious twist of fate, not only did the contemnors make reference to this heinous act in their discourse, their comments were made on the eve of the 34th anniversary of that act. Their comments therefore could not be easily dismissed as mere threats because it carried the weight of a ghastly past. How could pardoning such contemnors therefore be in the interest of the people of Ghana? Does the pardon not amount to a mockery of our own history and our resolve to preserve the independence of the judiciary if we celebrate Martyrs day yet fail to condemn the Montie trio for scandalizing the apex court, bringing its name into disrepute and threatening its officers?

We have so far proffered arguments accentuating the illegitimacy of the pardon power exercise by President Mahama. We need not overemphasize the fact that an independent judiciary is the backbone of rule of law in a democratic society such as ours. When there is an improper use of the pardon power, it undermines the confidence and belief of the citizens in the rule of law. We therefore need to have transparent and accountable mechanisms that will regulate the use of the pardon power lest, it becomes the private tool of grace for future presidents and their allies.

## V. The Way Forward

Perhaps, when a presidential power such as the prerogative of mercy becomes the dysfunctional tool in the president's toolkit, discarding it into the dustbin of constitutional amendment where it will no longer be problematic seems to be the way to go. However, we do not subscribe to such view. We propose that the administration of the pardon power should rather be streamlined to ensure that it is not subject to abuse or misuse. These guidelines should be written regulations engineered by the Council of State. The guidelines on the exercise of pardon power should be drafted either by the Council of State or a committee of experts commissioned by the Council of State. We propose the

Council of State because it is the body constitutionally charged with the duty to counsel the President in the performance of his functions. The Council also carries a level of independence that will facilitate it in carrying out its duties.

With regards to its counsel to the President on grant of pardon cases, the Council of State should function more like the Office of the Pardon Attorney (OPA) in the United States which is the recipient of all pardon applications. The OPA, upon receipt of the application conducts further investigations and makes its recommendations as to whether the President should grant pardon or not. The OPA then forwards its recommendation to the President. This procedure is preferable to the existing practice in Ghana, as contrasted with the happenings of the Montie trio case, where the President first received the petition for pardon and then forwarded the petition to the Council of State for consideration.

The Council of State like the Kenyan Advisory Committee on Prerogative of Mercy should also take into account the views of the victims of the offence when making its recommendations on the grant of pardon to the President. In the alternative, an independent Committee assigned specifically to the exercise of the prerogative of mercy should be set up as is the case in Kenya and the United States.

The above recommended regulations will make pardon a rare enterprise. Even though this power is vested only in the President, care should be taken so that it is not subjected to the President's whims and caprices. The pardon power should be administered to ensure that the power rightly serves its purpose of correcting injustices in the criminal justice system.

We are not by this suggesting that pardon should solely be an instrument of justice, in fact, it cannot. It is an instrument of mercy not instituted to be fair in the same sense that an equitable justice system is but it should ultimately be in the interest and welfare of the general public.[96] The pardon power should reassure the public of a power properly vested in the President and not incite fears of a power gone rogue. The judiciary will then have the power to review the exercise of the pardon power under certain circumstance as stipulated in the Indian case of Maru Ram supra.

The pardon power should also be a tool for advancing rather than interfering with the criminal justice system. Thus, when the pardon power is properly exercised, it will expose the flaws in the criminal justice system and cause a stir

---

96 Margaret Colgate Love, Reinventing the President's Pardon Power, Federal Sentencing Reporter Vol 20, No. 1 pp 5-15 October 2007.

which will lead to a consensus for restructuring. Even though the propriety of the exercise of the pardon power by President Mahama in the Montie trio case is questionable, it reveals the need for contempt of court under article 19(12) to be codified. Perhaps, if such codification of contempt ex facie curiae was in existence at the time, there will be a prescribed minimum and maximum term of imprisonment and the President could not have made claims concerning the "harshness" of the punishment. Codification of this offence is essential because first of all, it promotes certainty. Also, where the president exercises the grant of pardon regarding offences which are well regulated by written law, the President will have a yardstick to measure the extent to which the grant of pardon will be legitimate.

# 6

# STRENGTHENING STATE INSTITUTIONS AFTER 60 YEARS OF INDEPENDENCE. THE CASE OF THE COUNCIL OF STATE IN GHANA

Samuel. A. Adjei

Kwame Frimpong

**Abstract**

The Council of State is a body of both appointed and elected representatives constitutionally mandated to counsel the President of Ghana on matters of national importance. It first appeared in the Constitution of 1969 and subsequently maintained in the 1979 and 1992 Constitutions. It has the semblance of the traditional system of governance where a traditional ruler has a council of elders he consults for advice. As an institution of state, there have been several calls from a wider section of the general public, including legal practitioners, politicians and academics, suggesting that the Council of State be abolished because, it does not serve a very useful purpose in terms of offering any meaningful advice to the President. In other words, the Presidency can work smoothly without it. Others on the other hand, hold the view that the institution can be strengthened to fulfill the proper role that is envisaged for it. This paper therefore looks at the Council of State as an institution of state in Ghana, deriving its mandate from the 1992

Constitution, and considers its relevance in the current democratic system of governance. It explores the mandate, composition and remuneration of the council as well as the challenges associated with them. The paper proposes solutions to strengthen the Council of State by calling for a relook into the caliber and expertise of people on the council and the method through which they become members as well as how they conduct their day to day business. After 60 years of independence, an institution that is constitutionally mandated to aid and counsel the Head of State must have a stronger legal backing to make its advice binding on the presidency.

## 1.0 Introduction

On 6th March 2017, Ghana attained 60 years of political independence. 60 years in a life of a person is considered an age of maturity and wisdom. The country has therefore come a long way in governance, rule of law, human rights and development. One aspect of good governance after 60 years of attaining statehood is the proper functioning of state institutions since the vehicle through which good governance can be delivered is through strong state institutions.

The Political history of Ghana reveals how the country has had its fair share of strong men.[1] Now the focus is on building strong institutions,[2] thus, institutions not manipulated by any other person or organ of government. It is on this basis that the Council of State, which is the highest advisory body mandated by law to counsel the President will be discussed.

The Council of State came into existence with the beginning of Ghana's second republic. The institution was first created by Article 53 of the 1969 Constitution to aid and counsel the President. It consisted of the Prime Minister, the Speaker of the National Assembly, the leader of the opposition and the President of the National House of Chiefs among others.[3] It is worth noting that Ghana was practicing the parliamentary system of governance in 1969 with a Prime Minister and a ceremonial President. According to proposals by the Committee of Experts on a draft constitution for the country,

1 From the Days of the first republic when Ghana became a one party state to the various military regimes where the elements of democracy such as free and fair elections, rule of law were little or non-existent.
2 Former U.S President, Barack Obama noted in his speech in Accra in 2009 that Africa does not need strong men but strong institutions.
3 Constitution of the Republic of Ghana, 1969. Assembly Press

the institution was to "serve as a buffer institution between the Prime Minister and President, who may be of different political ideologies.

The Council of State continued to exist during the third republican as the Article 106 of the 1979 Constitution gave it effect. It is interesting to note that after a shift from the Parliamentary system of 1969 to the Presidential system of 1979, the primary function of the Council of State was also amended slightly. The Council of State was now to aid and counsel the President and Parliament in the performance of their respective functions. This is significant because in the third republic, the executive was strictly separated from the legislature, in that no Member of Parliament (MP) could double as a minister of State. Per Article 65 (2) of the 1979 Constitution, An MP appointed a Minister of State shall resign from Parliament before he assumes office. There was therefore the need for an advisory body to continue serving as a buffer institution between the executive and the legislature which were distinct from each other.

The current 1992 Constitution has lived longer than all the previous republican constitutions but less than half of 60 years. The Council of State is enjoined by Ghana's 1992 Constitution to counsel the President in the performance of his functions. The Council is required to consider and advise the President or any other authority in respect of any appointment which is required by the Constitution or any other law to be made in accordance with the advice of, or in consultation with the Council. A wider section of the general public have difficulties with the constitutional mandate, composition and remuneration of the Council of State[4]. According to the Constitution Review Commission report, some submissions called for the Council of State to be expanded into a Second House of Parliament. Such a House, they argued, would be capable of discussing Bills and other matters of national importance in a dispassionate and non-partisan manner in the supreme interest of the nation. An equal number of submissions called for the abolition of the Council of State. Those who held this view reasoned that the Council of State had outlived its usefulness and a third set of submissions took a middle course and called for the remodelling of the Council of State so that it is better able to perform its current constitutional functions.

This paper seeks to explore the difficulties with the constitutional mandate, composition and remuneration of the council and suggests solutions to surmount the challenges. The paper is divided into four (4) major headings;

4 See Report of the Constitution Review Commission submitted to President John Atta Mills on 20th December, 2011

the Introduction, Discussions, Solutions and Conclusion, with subheadings under the discussions.

## 2.0 Discussions

### 2.1 Issues arising from the mandate and functions of the Council of State

Article 89(1), 91(1) (2) (3) (4) of the 1992 Constitution, spells out the mandate of the Council of State. Aside from providing counsel to the president, the Council of State may, upon request or on its own initiative, consider and make recommendations on any matter being considered or dealt with by the President, a Minister of State, Parliament or any other authority established by this Constitution except that the President, Minister of State, Parliament or other authority shall not be required to act in accordance with any recommendation made by the Council of State.[5] They may also perform such other functions as may be assigned to it by the Constitution or any other law not inconsistent with the Constitution.

### 2.1.2 Is the President bound by the decisions of the Council of State?

There is some confusion on the issue of whether the decisions reached by the Council of State is binding on the President. In seeking clarity on the matter, it is imperative to throw light on two key phrases as used in Article 91(1). *On the advice of,* and *in consultation with.*

> 91.
> (1) The Council of State shall consider and advise the President or any other authority in respect of any appointment which is required by this Constitution or any other law to be made in accordance with the advice of, or in consultation with, the Council of State.
> (2) The advice referred to in clause (1) of this article shall be given not later than thirty days after the receipt of the request from the President or other authority.

The drafters of the Constitution sought to differentiate between the advisory and the consultation mandates of the Council of State which seems to suggest

5 See Article 91(3) of the 1992 Constitution

that the two are not the same in law. Article 70 (1) (2) uses both terms in different appointments.

70.

(1) The President shall, **acting in consultation** with the Council of State, appoint-

(a) the Commissioner for Human Rights and Administrative Justice and his Deputies;

(b) the Auditor-General;

(c) the District Assemblies Common Fund Administrator;

(d) the Chairmen and other members of -

(i) the Public Services Commission;

(ii) the Lands Commission;

(iii) the governing bodies of public corporations;

(iv) a National Council for Higher Education howsoever described; and

(e) the holders of such other offices as may be prescribed by this Constitution or by any other law not inconsistent with this Constitution.

(2) The President shall, **acting on the advice of** the Council of State, appoint the Chairman, Deputy Chairmen, and other members of the Electoral Commission.

Legal luminaries have sought to interpret these provisions to mean that where it is provided that the president shall *acting in consultation with*, means that the President is not bound by the advice of the Council of State and therefore may act contrary[6] and where it is stipulated that the president shall *acting on the advice of*, means that the President is bound by the advice of the Council of State and therefore cannot act to the contrary.[7]

6 Some provisions that mandates the President to act in consultation with the Council of State are: Article 70(1), Article 72 (1), Article 74(1), Article 144(1) (2), Article 146(6), Article 183(4a), Article 185(3), Article 186(1a) Article 189(1), Article 201(g), Article 202(1), Article 206(h), Article 207(1), Article 211(d), Article 212(1), Article 224

7 Kwamena Ahwoi explained this provision during a lecture on Public sector regulatory framework at GIMPA. Some provisions that mandates the President to act on the advice of the Council of State are: Article 5(2) (3), Article 70 (2), Article 31(1), Article 44(6), Article 146(4) (10 a), Article 187(8), Article 189(4), Article 232(2), Article 278(1b), Article 290(2), Article 291(2)

However, in the recent Supreme Court case of the GBA v AG[8] which was consolidated by two other jointly filed separate suits by applicants- Richard Dela Sky and Kwasi Danso Acheampong seeking an interpretation of Article 70 on whether or not the advice of the Council of State in the said appointments under Article 70(2) of the Constitution is binding on the President, the Supreme Court held that the advisory opinions of the Council of State is not binding on the President. This raises questions on the essence of the Council when their advice is not binding on the President.

### 2.1.3 Does the Council of State fit into the Current System of Government?

With Ghana currently practising the Executive Presidential system of government, some are convinced that the Council of State was operating in a vacuum because its very foundation was no more in existence.[9] Osei[10] notes that the institution was set up to mediate the political impasse between the President and Prime Minister, however, the current constitution has no provision for a split executive therefore no political impasse for the Council to resolve. In effect, with or without the Council of State, the Presidency can function smoothly.

Article 57 (1) (2) of the 1992 Constitution stipulates that there shall be a President of the Republic of Ghana who shall be the Head of State and Head of Government and Commander-in Chief of the Armed Forces of Ghana.

(2) The President shall take precedence over all other persons in Ghana; and in descending order, the Vice-President, the Speaker of Parliament and the Chief Justice, shall take precedence over all other persons in Ghana.

Even though the 1992 Constitution does not provide for the office of Prime Minister and therefore no political impasse for the Council of State to mediate between the President and the Prime Minister, the framers of the Constitution decided to maintain the institution to serve in a consultation and advisory capacity.

8 2016
9 He made the point at a 'Thought Leadership Debate' organised by Joy FM on the relevance of the institution
10 Junior partner with Kulendi @ Law

## 2.2 Issues Arising with the Composition of the Council of State.

Article 89(2) of the Constitution 1992, stipulates the members of the council of state and how they get on to the institution.

89 (2) The Council of State shall consist of -

> (a) the following persons appointed by the President in consultation with Parliament -
>> (i) one person who has previously held the office of Chief Justice;
>> (ii) one person who has previously held the office of Chief of Defence Staff of the Armed Forces of Ghana;
>> (iii) one person who has previously held the office of Inspector-General of Police;
> (b) the President of the National House of Chiefs;
> (c) one representative from each region of Ghana elected, in accordance with regulations made by the Electoral Commission under Article 51 of this Constitution, by an electoral college comprising two representatives from each of the districts in the region nominated by the District Assemblies in the region; and
> (d) eleven other members appointed by the President.

### 2.2.1 Rubber Stamp

Currently, the 1992 Constitution empowers the President to appoint 14 out of the 25 member council. A wider section of the public view the composition of the council as ineffective because majority of the members appointed are party loyalists and cannot act against the President who appointed them. Appointing majority of the members makes it a rubber stamp since you don't bite the hand that feeds you. Also, the current practice by which the Chairman of the Council of State is proposed by the President and almost automatically endorsed by the Council of State does not give it credibility in the eye of the public.[11] The Chairman of the Council has almost always turned out to be a known former active government functionary or surrogate in some powerful institution of state.[12]

11 See Report of the Constitution Review Commission submitted to President John Atta Mills on 20th December, 2011
12 The likes of Professor Kofi Awoonor, JHM Newman, Cecilia Johnson among others.

### 2.2.2 Inadequate Expertise on Certain Crucial Matters

The Council of State has come under severe criticism for not having enough experts to thoroughly advise the Head of State. This criticism came to a head when upon the advice of the Council of State, the then President John Mahama pardoned the "Montie 3" after they were convicted of contempt by the highest court of the land. A political science lecturer, Dr. Richard Amoako Baah asserted that members of the Council of State lacked the legal expertise to advise the president on remission for the Montie trio. According to Baah, there is a big flaw in the constitution to say that the Council of State can advise the president on some matters. Critical questions that arose included their expertise, whether  legal minds,  lawyers, constitutional expertise among others.[13]

### 2.2.3 Is It an All-Inclusive Membership?

The 1992 Constitution spells out how members should be appointed or elected to serve on the Council. However, the question on the mind of some people is whether the Council has an all -inclusive membership. Certainly on the political front, provisions was not made for former Presidents, opposition leaders or a clear percentage of women representation on the Council.

### 2.3 Issues Arising with the Remunerations of the Members of the Council of State

Article 89(7) of the Constitution 1992, spells out how the members of the Council of State are remunerated:

(7) The Chairman and members of the Council of State shall be entitled to such allowances and privileges as may be determined in accordance with Article 71 of this Constitution.

(8) The allowances and privileges of the Chairman and other members of the Council of State shall be charged on the Consolidated Fund and shall not be varied to their disadvantage while they hold office.

---

13 See http://www.abongobimedia.com/2016/08/24/council-of-state-is-rubber-stamp-dr-baah/

### 2.3.1 Drain on National Coffers

In the view of a section of the public, the Council of State is an irrelevant institution draining the national coffers. According to Osei, the cost incurred by the nation in running the Council of State was estimated to be GH¢15.6 million annually, which, he argued, could be better used to provide social amenities across the country.[14] The Council of State has recently come under intense public scrutiny following the revelation that each member is paid some GH¢13,000 monthly to give advice which is not binding on the President.[15] Since the allowances and privileges shall not be varied to their disadvantage while they hold office there is a perception that the allowances members of the Council of State enjoy are always adjusted upwards to their advantage.

Those calling for the abolition of the Council of State acknowledge the fact that it is constitutionally mandated to be in existence; but when they consider how ineffective the Constitution itself is, they pause to ponder whether this Council is worth the expenditure that is made to sustain it.

### 3.0 Proposed Solutions

The culture of bastardizing state institutions without proposing solutions to help strengthen them is not the best. Before calling for a dissolution of the council, solutions must first be proffered and where the solutions do not work then other measures can be taken. Ghana is not the only country having a Council of State. Nigeria, Portugal, and the Republic of Ireland all have a Council of State as an advisory body to the Head of State.

Rather than scrapping the institution, Kojo Bentsil-Enchill[16] has argued that the Council must be strengthened to be able to deliver on its mandate, adding that some interventions by the Council, he believed, accounted for the peace and unity in the country. He bemoaned the destructive tendencies of Ghanaians, arguing that such state institutions require the support of the citizenry to be able to function appropriately.

It is worthy of note that the Constitution Review Commission report have made some recommendations to strengthen the Council of State. The

14 See http://www.abongobimedia.com/2017/02/03/abolish-council-of-state-lawyer/
15 See http://www.myjoyonline.com/politics/2017/February-17th/council-of-state-was-abused-under-mahama-okudzeto.php?utm_source=dlvr.it&utm_medium=facebook
16 Senior Partner, Bentsil-Enchill, Letsa and Ankomah Law Firm

Commission recommends that the Council of State should be maintained as an advisory body to the President, the Parliament, the Judiciary and other critical institutions of state on issues of national importance.

It also recommended that the Council of State should present annual reports to Parliament for review, discussion and debate and for Parliament to consider enacting a legislation that provides for the functions, funding, accounting and annual reporting of the Council of State.

Again, the Commission recommends strongly that the members of the Council of State should maintain their independence and neutrality at all times and should not take part in active party politics and that the current practice by which the Chairman of the Council of State is proposed by the President and almost automatically endorsed by the Council of State be discontinued. Instead, the Council of State should independently select its own Chairperson.

Building on these recommendations by the Constitution Review Commission, we also propose that, in order for the Council of State to stay relevant, it must open itself to media coverage of its modus operandi. The Council may have acted in diplomacy to build consensus to dissuade the President on unwise decisions but because they are not open to the public, it is difficult to assess the good sides of the institution. It is clear in Article 92 (3) that the Council of States shall hold its meetings in camera but may admit the public to any meetings whenever it considers it appropriate. The Council of State needs to be more open to the public whose taxes are used to pay them. It is unfortunate to note that the Council has no website that can promote their activities and publish some of their reports for public consumption. We don't even know who speaks for them. A public relations unit must therefore be established or if it is existent, should be strengthened to be able to have frequent interactions with the general public on the mandate, success and challenges of the institution. Some of their meetings should be broadcasted for the public to have confidence in their institutions.

Furthermore, a critical institution like the Council of State must be equipped with adequate resources to enable the effective performance of its functions. President Akufo Addo revealed during the inauguration of the current Council of State that the Council's building is in a deplorable state and they have no Chief Director.

Finally and more importantly, there is an urgent need to take a second look at the composition of the members of the Council of State. 25 member council whose advice is not binding on the Presidency is not value for money. We propose the cutting down of the number so as to cut down the drain on the national coffers.

Also, for the sake of inclusiveness, we propose that leaders of opposition parties represented in Parliament must be de facto members of the Council of State as well as surviving Heads of State. In Nigeria for example, the Council of State, the highest constitutional advisory body, includes all past Presidents and Heads of States.[17]

## 4.0 Conclusion

Ghana is not the only country that has a Council of State. Nigeria, Portugal, and the Republic of Ireland all have a Council of State as an advisory body to the Head of State.

After 60 solid years of independence, state institutions must function effectively in order to promote good governance and build public confidence in institutions rather that running them down. The view that the outcome of consultations of the President with the Council of State is not binding on the President fuels public perception that it is an irrelevant institution. The Constitution 1992, must therefore be amended in order to give very clear guidelines as to what provisions are binding on the President and what provisions are not.

17 See http://www.premiumtimesng.com/news/154595-update-obasanjo-buhari-absent-nigerias-council-state-endorses-national-conference.html

# 7

# POOR RECORDS MANAGEMENT AND THE MOCKERY OF JUSTICE IN GHANA

## Thomas Appiah Kubi Asante

**Abstract**

The administration of justice greatly relies on records. The Data Protection Act, 2012 (Act 843) enhances record management. The fundamental basis for Ghana's data protection law is Article 18 (2) of the 1992 Constitution, which guarantees individual privacy except for public safety or the economic well-being of the country, for the protection of health or morals, for the prevention of disorder or crime or for the protection of the rights or freedoms. The rampant incidents of missing dockets at the various courts in the country have been of grave concern to members of the Bar and the judiciary has been advised to find lasting solutions because absence of records hampers justice delivery in Ghana. However, poor records management is not the only factor contributing to slow and ineffective justice system in Ghana. Inaccurate record keeping would often lead to the miscarriage of justice in Ghana. This paper advocates for the use of biometric readers, which can help identify the profile of criminals and accused persons. This can expose people who stand sureties for a number of accused with false identities.

## Introduction

Records and justice are inseparable. The inseparability of the two concepts is manifested even in the origin of the term "record" itself. The term record originally denotes the written documents kept by a court as evidence of its proceedings (Kirkwood, 1996, p. 1). Poyser and Milne (2011) posit that justice can never be miscarriage-free, but records can mitigate the miscarriage of justice.

The need for records management is enhanced by the Data Protection Act, 2012 (Act 843). The fundamental basis for Ghana's data protection law is Article 18 (2) of the 1992 Constitution which guarantees the following: 'No person shall be subjected to interference with the privacy of his home, property, correspondence or communication except in accordance with law and as may be necessary in a free and democratic society for public safety or the economic well-being of the country, for the protection of health or morals, for the prevention of disorder or crime or for the protection of the rights or freedoms of others.'

The Data Protection Act set up the Data Protection Commission (DPC) and provided for the process by which personal data can be obtained and used in order to guarantee Article 18(2). This Act imposes a duty on the state to ensure that administrative action is lawful, reasonable and procedurally fair and that everyone whose rights have been adversely affected by administrative action has the right to be given written reasons for such an action. A person who is of the opinion that his/her rights have been materially and adversely affected by administrative action may request that he/she be provided with reasons for such an action.

The Ghana Bar Association (GBA) has expressed serious concern about the rampant incidents of missing dockets at the various courts in the country. These were contained in a Resolution passed at the end of the 2017-2018 conference held by members of the Bar at Sunyani in the Brong Ahafo region in September, and signed by its National President and National Secretary, Benson Nutsukpui and Justin Agbeli Amenuvor. The Bar, therefore, urged the Judicial Service to ensure that the Registrars of the various courts take steps to effectively monitor movements of dockets and also to be proactive in generating temporary dockets, where necessary, to facilitate expeditious determination of cases.

Absence of records hampers justice delivery in Ghana. The absence of records could be due to missing dockets, missing documents etc by assigned officials who are designated to keep and produce them at a court of competent jurisdiction. For instance, most media houses reported on January 5, 2018 with the banner headline "J.B Danquah autopsy report missing – Pathologist tells court". Dr. Lawrence Edusei, the pathologist who conducted a post mortem on the late Member of Parliament, J.B Danquah, has said that he lost the autopsy report after a burglary at his residence in September 2016. This was after the presiding judge, Her Worship Arit Nsemoh ordered him to appear before the court and explain why the autopsy report was not ready.

After being asked how long it would take to prepare a new report, Dr. Edusei stated that he was not certain on the period of time within which he could prepare a new autopsy report. The pathologist explained that writing the autopsy report was going to be an additional work of getting access to pictures taken during the post mortem, recollecting everything he saw and putting it into writing again. This is a matter of concern to this writer as he sees that poor record keeping could derail or cause travesty of justice in Ghana.

## Problem statement

Nobody can underestimate the importance of proper and good records keeping in our judicial and justice delivery system in Ghana. The importance of proper records management seems to have rarely been identified as a factor in ensuring administration of justice in Ghana. Poor records management can affect the administration and delivery of justice, and efficient administration of justice cannot be expected in an environment where records are difficult to retrieve or are susceptible to loss. The consequences are that cases are delayed or stalled which, in effect, means that justice is delayed or denied, leading to loss of faith in the judicial system.

In Ghana, many cases reported to the Ghana Police Service are withdrawn or do not end up in court neither is arbitration used to settle it nor stakeholders express disinterest but it is due to issues and reasons such as missing dockets, lack of supporting documents or people not volunteering necessary information to the police or the prosecutor on time, leading to adjournment, postponement and discontinuation of cases.

In other instances, investigating officers have been known to remove the comments of other officers from dockets (World Bank and International Records Management Trust, 2002). Furthermore, missing documents and case records are common in remanded cases. In Ghana, people have been in prison remand custody for over a decade with the flimsy excuse that either their dockets are missing or the investigator have passed on or have been transferred. Records are not produced in the courts of law at the time when required for justice to prevail, leading justice to be either denied or delayed. Prosecutors also take case records home to work on them outside office hours, and this might lead to these case records being lost or even sold by the prosecutors, e.g. Percy Yutar, the prosecutor in the Rivonia trial who sold some of the records of the trial to the Brenthurst Library in Britain.

As research has shown, the chaotic state of public records in many countries makes it virtually impossible to determine responsibility for official actions and to hold individuals accountable for their actions. This failure to manage records properly has been a contributory factor to the growing menace of corruption in the running of public affairs and the loss of public confidence in the justice system of Ghana. There is widespread perception of corruption, undue delays and inexperienced judicial officers taking place across the country.

## Purpose and Objectives of the Study

The purpose of this paper was to investigate how poor records management affects the administration of justice delivery in Ghana. The specific objectives were to:

- Investigate the contribution of records management to the justice system in Ghana.
- Identify cases of delayed or denied justice relating to record-keeping in the justice system (Missing Dockets in Ghana)

## Records and Provision of Justice

An uncountable number of scholars and writers have laid emphasis and echoed the important roles of how good records management helps in the administration of justice worldwide. Mentions can be made of Abioye (2014), Lowry (2012), Mukembo (2000), Poyser and Milne (2011), Saurombe (2014), who have written about the role of records management in the provision of justice. Indeed, in many ways, records and justice are inseparable concepts. Mukembo (2000) reports that in Uganda, management of records is in a pathetic state, leading to delay in administering of justice. He cites corruption among some judicial officers and the police as some of challenges relating to failure of the justice system. Other factors include misfiling of police dockets. Mukembo (2000) estimates that "once in a while, the court process will be brought to a standstill because a file is lost or missing". He adds that sometimes files are misplaced or sometimes stolen or they vanish, and the disappearance is usually more dramatic in the courts of law and the police department. An issue of grave concern in many countries is one of poorly managed records having a negative impact on the provision of justice (Motsaathebe and Mnjama, 2009b). This concern was also echoed by remarks made by Redelinghuys in court that "clerks' incompetence had caused about 50 to 60 case records to be lost, stolen or destroyed in the past three years" (Mail and Guardian, 2011). Furthermore, delays in obtaining results from institutions such as the hospital laboratories, food and drugs authorities, Ghana Standard Authority etc causing bottlenecks in the criminal justice system in many parts of Ghana. These delays could result in hundreds of prisoners convicted of serious crimes, including murder, being freed due to bureaucratic bungling. When the prisoners make appeals and their transcripts cannot be furnished due to inaccessible, lost or stolen case records, their rights to access to information and to appeals are infringed. As a result, the prisoners could be set free because of the officials' negligence and the ineffectiveness of records management in the Judicial Service of Ghana. This also infringed the rights of the victims of protection from the offenders by the justice system due to officials' inappropriate handling of case records.

Records represent a major source of information and are almost the only reliable and legally verifiable data source that can serve as evidence of decisions, actions and transactions in the public service, as opposed to oral evidence (Barata et al., 2000; Wamukoya, 2000). This is also emphasized by Force (2013, p. 25) when he suggested that written records are more trustworthy than oral evidence. Motsaathebe and Mnjama (2009a) contend that records provide the most critical evidence in court. Records as evidence therefore underpin all relationships, whether social, legal, moral or business. Therefore, governments need to maintain accurate and reliable records as a tool to ensure just and fair treatment of their citizens.

The International Records Management Trust (IRMT) (1999, p. 8) adds that when records are not produced at the right time, a fair judgment is denied on the side of both the offender and the government. This is information that a records management practitioners should be able to provide. In other words, records professionals should know when an original has been destroyed and when the original is available (Force, 2013, p. 127). Therefore, if reliable records are not maintained, it becomes very difficult for the court to pass judgment or make a decision, resulting in the public losing faith in its government (Valtonen, 2007). As a result, records need to be managed properly to accelerate the delivery of justice (Lowry, 2012). Legal records provide evidence of contractual obligations, duties and privileges agreed upon by governments, organisations or individuals. They provide a record of matters such as property titles, charitable status and other legal and civil rights. Hounsome (2001, p. 1) noted that although records management may be regarded as just a mere filing, it plays a tremendous role in the provision of justice. According to him, records management objectives usually fall into one of following three categories:

1. Service (effective and efficient);
2. Profit (or cost-avoidance); and
3. Social (moral, ethical and legal) responsibility.

Failure to manage records properly would be one of the biggest stumbling blocks and catastrophic to an efficient Ghanaian justice system and lead to miscarriage of justice delivery in our entire judiciary.

According to Katuu (2015), while the use of technology through computerized records has been touted as a possible panacea to the problem of poor records management (Seedat *et al.*, 2003), experiences in more developed countries such the UK (Benson, 2001) have demonstrated that computerisation is neither easy nor always successful. In Ghana, one of the most prominent projects is the implementation of automation or the leveraging of ICT in our judicial system to harness proportionate technology to improve the efficiency of legal procedures that are too often cumbersome and paper-based, leading to confusion, delay and miscarriage of justice (Saurombe, 2014). However, despite the availability of the system, some cases are still reported to be withdrawn due to lack of integrity of data. Furthermore, the system is not integrated with the system used by the police and correctional services.

**Scope and Research Methodology**

To undertake a content analysis of cases of denied or delayed justice as a results of poor records management, this paper extracted data from the Ghanaian media both newspapers and websites of media houses on cases related to record-keeping and miscarriage of justice published in newspapers.

**Examples of Missing Dockets in Ghana**

Cases of missing dockets in courts are not rare in Ghana.

## A-G's 'Missing Docket' Pops Up!

A docket on the case in which a 22-year-old man is being tried for strangulating a seven-year-old girl to death has resurfaced at the Attorney-General's Department months after it mysteriously disappeared.

Francisca Tutu Mensah, a Principal State Attorney, told an Accra Central Magistrate Court that the file got lost at the A-G's Department although it was forwarded to the State Prosecutor.

She stated that the Director for Public Prosecution (DPP), on the advice of the AG, had instructed her to take a two-week adjournment to commit the accused for trial.

Ms. Mensah disclosed that the accused, Lucas Agboyie, aka Gabriel or Kojo, a mason apprentice would be tried summarily for defilement.[1]

## Missing Docket Found

The docket which became a bone of contention between the Attorney-General (A-G) and the Director of the Bureau of National Investigation (BNI) has finally been found.

Contrary to earlier claims that the docket which was created for the prosecution of Mr. Nicholas Sakyi, an accountant at the Department of Urban Roads, Kumasi, was with the BNI, it had rather been found resting peacefully in a folder in the office of the A-G.

Mr. Sakyi was alleged to have embezzled ¢4.3 billion withholding tax deductions.[2]

## Judgment on Two Year Case Postponed Due to Missing Docket

Two litigants who turned up at the James Town Magistrate Court in Accra for judgment in their case had to leave in anger and frustration after they were told that the docket on the case was missing.

The case had been in the court since February 2012 and had travelled through the process until judgment was due, but the magistrate had to call the two parties to her chambers to find an amicable solution after the registrar had reported that the docket was nowhere to be found.

1 https://www.modernghana.com/news/724536/a-gs-missing-docket-pops-up.html
2 Daily Guide, October 26, 2007

A source told the Daily Graphic that the magistrate, Ms. Grace Gunugu, in the absence of the docket, prevailed on the parties to reach a consensus on three options — the case starts afresh, the two parties supply their copies of the proceedings for the case to continue or they petition the Chief Justice.

The parties were given two weeks within which to arrive at a decision.[3]

## Missing dockets of the past

### September 5, 2007

The docket on a case in which a Kumasi Magistrate Court ordered that the employers of a journalist, Mark Bunde, pay his severance package, was reported missing when he applied for a writ to attach his employers properties.

### October 22, 2007

The docket of the case in which Charles Quansah was convicted for killing 34 women went missing from the registries of the High Court and the Court of Appeal. His appeal stalled because the docket could not be found. The docket later resurfaced.

### August 16, 2011

The docket on popular hip life musician Mzbel who was charged with offences including unauthorized parking, resisting arrest and assault on a police officer went missing.

### December 20, 2011

The docket on the controversial cocaine-turned-soda case involving DSP Gifty Tehoda was reported missing.[4]

## Discussion

This section presents and discusses the findings of the content analysis of newspaper articles relating to record-keeping and justice in Ghana.

Most of the issues raised in the article relate to missing dockets, court records and lack of supporting documentation with a few dealing with tampered evidence. As a result, cases were either dismissed or postponed, resulting in the travesty of justice. Some of the court cases are still pending, as there is no evidence. It is clear that the police stations, courts and correctional services are responsible for the loss of records.

3 Daily Graphic, July 8, 2014
4 Graphic Online

Interviews with the police officers indicate that there are two ways of registering a case. A police officer either goes to the crime scene to take evidence and then register a case or the victim visits the police station and opens a case. The case is firstly registered manually and then entered onto the system. According to the participant:

Usually, human error contributes to the docket getting missing or stolen. For example, after opening a case manually, the police officer can be distracted and forget a case on the counter and somebody might misplace it. If that happens before it is captured on the system, it might never be recovered. Once the docket is missing, the case is provisionally withdrawn, but is not taken out of the system. In the past, it was very easy for a case to be stolen because it was registered manually on a paper-based system and it was not easy to detect if it is stolen. But, now a person can only change the wording on the system only because if she/he deletes the case on the system, it will still be retrieved from the back-up system.

However, in some cases, it can be as a result of corrupt police officers or officials who make a docket or documents in the docket disappear. In a report by Corruption Watch on myjoyonline it was reported that on 29ᵗʰ August, 2018 some unidentified persons have been staging frequent break-ins at the offices of the Ministry of Justice and Attorney-General in Accra. One of the topmost officers affected is the Director of Public Prosecutions, Yvonne Attakorah Obuobisa, whose office was broken into in March 2018. In that incident, the burglars took away a laptop computer and a printer.

It is unclear the sort of documents and programmes that were installed on the computer and whether they have any consequences on cases that the Attorney-General's office is prosecuting or studying. Sources say there have been further break-ins at the offices occupied by the Chief Director of the Ministry of Justice and a state attorney as well as the Drafting Department.

In the break-in of the Chief Director's office, a television set was stolen. A state attorney also had her office burgled, losing one laptop computer. In the last incident that happened on 28ᵗʰ August, 2018, *Corruption Watch* investigated, the Drafting Office lost a total of three laptop computers in two incidents.

Together, five laptop computers, one printer and a television set are the items that the burglars have taken away so far in the series of break-ins.

The unknown perpetrators usually do not tamper with the doors and windows during their operations.

Furthermore, a joint report by World Bank and Norwegian Ministry of Foreign Affairs (2010) in Ethiopia reveals that a certain amount of police corruption contributes to loss of records as police can be paid to ignore a crime, overlook evidence against the major suspect, or alternatively to fabricate a case for pay.

The implication of missing dockets is that it weakens the case and gives a bad image to the justice system. The docket contains the source documents, without which it could very well be that the matter will not proceed. However, it is possible a matter can proceed in its absence if copies are available. If court records are not accurate there might be serious implications as well. However, an original piece of evidence, particularly a document, is superior to a copy and if the original is available, a copy will not be allowed as evidence in a trial.

The discussions indicated that lack of skills in properly managing records also contributes to dockets and court records being missing. This is so because current records are not managed by qualified personnel but by the police officers themselves. As a result, the police officers can take the dockets home, lose them there or even sell them to make a case disappear. This is not unique to the justice system, as Ngoepe (2012) argues that in the South African public sector, records management practitioners are relegated to the periphery of the public sector administration and most records are managed only during their last stage when they metamorphosed into archives and by then it is too late to control the records. Ngoepe's assertion on South Africa can equally be situated in Ghana's Public Sector Administration.

Failure to manage records can lead to the build-up of unwanted records, overcrowding and disorganisation. This, in turn, will make it very difficult to retrieve and use legal records efficiently and to carry out the justice system. The other dilemma is that some records (court, financial records, personnel records, electronic records and others) usually fall outside the jurisdiction of the organisation's records manager (Ngoepe and Ngulube, 2014). As a result, these records are not managed or controlled adequately. Furthermore, most managers do not rank organising records highly among their priorities. Instead, it is thought to be a mundane chore with which management should not be concerned. This tedious task is often left to the discretion of the staff in charge of records management (International Records Management Trust, 1999).

When records are missing, most of the time, the person who benefits from such a situation is the defendant, while the plaintiff suffers the injustice. A criminal justice system that consistently fails to secure convictions has little credibility and the danger exists that victims may stop reporting crime and communities may instead resort to extra-legal or vigilante action as what happened to Major Mahama (a Military Officer) who was killed by the youth of Denkyira Obuasi in the Central Region of Ghana.

## Conclusion

It is undeniable fact that records management is not the only factor contributing to slow, poor and effective justice system in Ghana, this paper indicated a strong association of poor record-keeping and the miscarriage of justice in Ghana with classical examples outside. This is due to the fact that the cases identified in this paper were either withdrawn, dismissed or postponed due to lack of or missing dockets. Even in the cases where a case continued without the docket justice was not served as offenders were set free while the plaintiff suffers the injustice. If court and police records are not accurate there might be serious implications such as withdrawal of case leading to travesty of justice. If records are not accounted for, lawyers, prosecutors and magistrates could dispute the authenticity of records. As a result, justice for victims would be delayed and ultimately denied while the perpetrators are freed. Therefore, effective management of records contributes to quick administration of justice, as records provide information through which evidence is derived and decisions made. Records need to be managed by qualified people in the area of records management rather than leaving the responsibility in the hands of police officers and magistrates. The use of biometric profiles of the accused, sureties, witnesses and other court users can be kept in an online databank. The use of biometric readers can help identify the profile of criminals and accused persons. This can expose people who stand sureties for a number of accused with false identities.

# 8

# 'I AM INDEPENDENT BUT I SPEAK MY MASTER'S TONGUE': A PARADOX OF INDEPENDENCE AND THE NEED TO TRANSLATE THE CONSTITUTION INTO GHANAIAN LANGUAGES

## Brian S. Akrong

**Abstract**

Ghana is a country enriched with diverse ethnicities with its attended variety in Ghanaian languages. Ghana attained independence in 1957 after years of colonial rule by the British and in 1960 attained its republican status. After the attainment of independence, Ghana elected to use the English language as its official language of communication. Since 1957, Ghana has had four Republics due to coup d'états. The 1992 Constitution of Ghana, the current Constitution, requires the promotion of Ghanaian languages and culture. Majority of Ghanaians cannot read and write in the English language. Therefore, this paper argues that until the 1992 Constitution is translated into the various Ghanaian languages, the section of the Ghanaian population who cannot read nor write in English have been disenfranchised and that is an abuse of their fundamental human rights.

## Introduction

The preamble to the 1992 Constitution of Ghana states that '...We the people of Ghana, in exercise of our natural and inalienable right to establish a framework of government which shall secure for ourselves and posterity the blessings of liberty, equality and prosperity....' The reference to 'the people of Ghana' has an underlying presumption of equality and participation that is based on the social contract theory. This theory is echoed further in the 'right to establish a framework of government.' The implications of these key words in the preamble are discussed below.

## Discussion of the Key Words in the Preamble of the 1992 Constitution

1. The Implications of Liberty:

The Longman dictionary of Contemporary English defines liberty as 'the freedom and the right to do whatever you want without asking permission or being afraid of authority.' John Stuart Mill (1859) explains that civil or social liberty refers to 'the nature and limits of the power which can be legitimately exercised by society over the individual' (Mill, 1859, p.6). Civil liberty historically was meant to set limits to the scope of authority or power which a ruler should exercise over his subjects (Mill, 1859). Mills (ibid) identified two means by which liberty was secured. The first was 'by obtaining recognition of certain immunities called political liberties or rights' (p.6). If a ruler infringed this liberty of its subjects or citizens, 'specific resistance, or general rebellion, was held to be justifiable' (Mill, 1859, p.7).

The second means of securing liberty 'was the establishment of constitutional checks, by which the consent of the community, or of a body of some sort, supposed to represent its interests, was made a necessary condition to some of the more important acts of the governing power' (Mills, 1859, p.7). The provision for liberty in the 1992 Constitution of Ghana is similar to the latter means of securing liberty as outlined by J.S Mill. The consent of the Ghanaian community to the provisions in the Constitution is presumed by the following clause in the preamble: 'We the People of Ghana, IN EXERCISE of our natural and inalienable right to establish a framework of government'. Yet, if the Constitution is not readily available to the people or even in a language they can read and understand, they may not be aware that they have any 'natural and inalienable right' to exercise or that it has been exercised on their behalf.

Article 12 of the 1992 Constitution provides that the fundamental human rights and freedoms enshrined in chapter five of the Constitution 'shall be respected and upheld' by all arms of government and 'all other organs of government and its agencies.' This in essence shall ensure liberty if citizens understand and are aware of the provision, and conduct themselves appropriately within the confines of the law. Additionally, Article 14 of the constitution provides for the protection of personal liberty and 'every person shall be entitled to his personal liberty' therefore 'no person shall be deprived of his personal liberty except…in accordance with procedure permitted by law.' Hence, liberty to citizens may be ensured if the citizens can read the legal provisions in the Constitution in a language they understand.

2. Life:

Basically, every individual is entitled to his life and this cannot be taken away from him or her as provided for in Article 13 of the 1992 Constitution. Article 13(1) of the 1992 Constitution specifically states that a person shall not be deprived of his life intentionally unless the person is convicted for a criminal offence, which merits death. For instance, a person who recklessly disregards the life of another and causes the death of that other person shall be liable to death as provided for under Sections 46, 49 and 49A of the Criminal Code, 1960 (Act 29). Section 46 of Act 29 specifically provides that, 'Whoever commits murder shall be liable to suffer death.' If these provisions are translated into Ghanaian languages, there may be better care as far as the life of another person is concerned. This understanding, for instance, may help to curb the spate of road accidents in Ghana.

3. Prosperity:

Article 18 of the 1992 Constitution provides for the right to own property. Every citizen or person legally residing within the country 'has the right to own property either alone or in association with others.' On the other hand, citizens must be aware that if they violate the law, their home, property or correspondence can be interfered with. This has to be read and understood by citizens, particularly those who are not able to proceed academically, who cannot read and write English properly but want to live luxuriously through various dubious means in the name of doing business. Such people should be able to read at least in a Ghanaian language to understand that cheating, stealing or duping people will lead to their right to property being interfered with. They should understand that in such an event legal action can be taken against them, inter alia, 'for the protection of health or morals, for the prevention of disorder or crime or for the protection of the rights or freedoms of others' (Article 18 (2)).

Notwithstanding these key fundamental rights mentioned in the preamble, language, whether verbal or brail, is a major means by which human rights can be enjoyed or denied because language is the vehicle of communication. If citizens can read and understand the contents of the constitution and other statutes, they may be able to enjoy their rights but when they are clouded by non-access and ignorance, the anticipation that citizens will enjoy their rights may be a mirage. In that case, the Latin maxim, 'nemo est supra leges' (no one is above the law) becomes a dream since those who do not know their basic rights may be trampled upon by others. It is not only the translation of the 1992 Constitution that matters but making it known to the populace that there is legal aid available to people, who cannot afford legal fees is also necessary.

It has been argued that claw back clauses are hindrances to the enjoyment of the full benefits from laws, which are intended to protect human rights. The 'implications of these claw-back clauses has a debilitating impact on the protection and promotion of human rights on the African continent' (Mapuva, 2016, p.1). In a similar vein, to have a constitution in a language which the majority of the people cannot read is to preserve a testament in a monastery remote from its beneficiaries.

A paradox is defined by McMahan et al. (1989) as 'an apparently contradictory statement that nonetheless makes sense' (p. 1093). Thus, Ghanaians have political independence, yet the laws are codified in the language of the colonial master; in effect, true independence is not attained when citizens cannot enjoy their rights to the fullest. Therein lies the paradox. Available records indicate that the Ghana Institute of Linguistics, Literacy and Bible Translation (GILBT) has assisted in the translation of an abridged version of the Constitution into twenty- four languages in the Northern part of Ghana (GNA, 2002) but even these cannot be found on the market. Besides, the number twenty-four is woefully inadequate because there are eighty-one (81) languages in Ghana (Lewis et al. 2017).

This paper considers the need to translate the Constitution into many Ghanaian languages as a post- colonial enterprise, which aims at decolonising the law; not in terms of watering down the time- tested tradition of legal language but making the law accessible to the ordinary citizen. It is also a human rights issue. If the citizens cannot read and understand the contents of the constitution, they are not likely to claim their rights under it.

Post-colonialism, as a literary movement, frowns upon the marginalisation or exclusion of non-Western traditions and forms of cultural life and expression (Selden & Widdowson, 1993). Western education appears to exclude those who cannot read and write from participating meaningfully in their nation's democracy. Hence, those who do not have the privilege of reading the Constitution either in English or any Ghanaian language are technically precluded from truly enjoying their rights. In effect, their effective participation in a system of democracy, which has the rule of law as its pillar, cannot be guaranteed. To exclude some people technically from the operations of the law implies that they are marginalised or excluded from fully participating in the national democratic process and the nation's march towards development. This is a situation which post-colonialism frowns upon.

It is appropriate that after sixty years of independence Ghanaians must reflect, *inter alia*, on legal issues that are crucial for the nation's meaningful existence and development. For as Socrates, the famous Greek Philosopher (c.469-399 B.C.) stated, 'The unexamined life is not worth living for man' (Grube, 2000). Examining this aphorism through a legal lens, one may say that a nation in pursuit of development must intermittently and critically examine legal issues which will promote its development. Likewise, Gyekye (2004, p.70) looking at the significance of individual and national periodic evaluation has stated that, 'Man cannot but philosophise, that is, pose fundamental questions, and reflect on fundamental aspects of human existence.' Hence, an assessment or evaluation of Ghana's democratic governance at the nation's attainment of sixty years is critical. Man cannot live by chance or upon the assumption that it shall be well by merely trusting himself or herself without responding to contemporary needs of the individual and society. This is why the understanding of the constitution is essential for citizens in a dynamic state.

Laws constitute the bedrock of orderliness and proper development. Glanville Williams (2002, p.2) stipulates that 'Law is the cement of society, and an essential medium of change' and enjoins us 'to think of the law as forming an integral part of a constantly evolving social landscape.' This implies that a better knowledge or understanding of the law will bring about desirable changes in the Ghanaian society. If the constitution is translated into several Ghanaian languages to afford citizens the opportunity to read and understand its contents, their knowledge of the law will increase their understanding of public affairs and give them a better understanding of social values (Williams, 2002, p.2). Citizens do not need to study the law as if they were law students but to capture a general understanding of the provisions of the constitution so as to know what to do and what not to do.

In a society, according to the social contract theory, people agree to co-exist in harmony by agreeing to fulfil certain moral as well as social obligations which they place upon themselves. Thomas Hobbes, John Locke and Jean –Jacque Rousseau are credited as famous proponents of the social contract theory (Internet Encyclopedia of Philosophy). In the modern democratic state, the constitution provides the framework for a social and democratic contract. In Ghana's 1992 constitution for instance, the rights and duties of citizens are provided for particularly in Chapter Five while the obligations of the government are also spelt out at various parts of the constitution. According to Jean-Jacque Rousseau (1762) each person in a society sacrifices his or her absolute freedom for the common good of all the members of the society. Rousseau explains the 'social compact' as follows:

> *Each of us puts his person and all his power in common under the*
> *supreme direction of the general will, and, in our corporate capacity,*
> *we receive each member as an indivisible part of the whole.* Rousseau
> (1762, p.7)

The relevance of indigenous Ghanaian languages not only as media of communication but also as conduits of democracy is reflected in Article 9 (2) of the 1992 Ghanaian Constitution, which stipulates that, 'Except as otherwise provided in Article 7…a person shall not be registered as a citizen of Ghana unless at the time of his application for registration he is able to speak and understand an indigenous language of Ghana.' Citizenship, certainly, traverses the ability to speak and understand a Ghanaian language. It should also imply the ability to read and understand the constitution and other coded statutes in Ghanaian language to be able to participate fully as a citizen in the democracy. Indeed, Article 39 (3) of the 1992 Constitution specifies that, 'The state shall foster the development of Ghanaian languages and pride in Ghanaian culture.' However, nowhere in the Constitution is it mentioned that the Constitution shall be translated into Ghanaian languages. This gap maybe considered a lacuna, which could be remedied to give legal backing to the translation enterprise.

Anyidoho (2009) in a review of human rights discourses in Ghana affirms that the 1992 Constitution of Ghana 'forms the bedrock for human rights in Ghana, and is supported by other national laws, as well as by international human rights instruments to which Ghana is signatory' (p.7). Incidentally, though various parts of the Constitution underscore the importance of human rights and the whole of Chapter Five is devoted to human rights, there is no mention that the Constitution should be translated into Ghanaian languages as a means of promoting human rights. Anyidoho (2009) focused on 'the evolution of human rights discourses and practices in Ghana' since the nation returned to constitutional rule in January 1993 (p.5). Additionally, the study focused on civil society organisations in view of their roles at the vanguard of the promotion of human rights in Ghana.

Chapter Five of the Constitution is devoted to the fundamental human rights and freedoms of Ghanaian citizens and Article 12 specifically provides that the rights and freedoms of individuals shall be upheld by all the arms of government and other organs and agencies as well as 'all natural and legal persons in Ghana.' If the Constitution is translated into several Ghanaian languages which the citizens can read and understand, they will know that whenever their rights are abused they can resort to the court and not take the law into their own hands because their rights 'shall be enforced by the courts as provided for in this Constitution' (Article 12 (1). Where they cannot afford legal fees, they should be made aware through radio stations which transmit in local languages that they can seek the services of the Legal Aid Board as provided for under Article 294 of the Constitution. This provision states that 'a person is entitled to legal aid in connection with any proceedings relating to this Constitution if he has reasonable grounds for taking , defending, prosecuting or being a party to the proceedings' (Article 294 (1) ). It is further provided in Article 294 (4) that 'legal aid shall consist of representation by a lawyer, including all such assistance as is given by a lawyer, in the steps preliminary or incidental to any proceedings or arriving at or giving effect to a compromise to avoid or to bring to an end any proceedings.' Due to poverty and ignorance the rights of some citizens may be trampled upon but this may be avoided or minimised if they can read in a Ghanaian language and understand what they should do to defend their rights notwithstanding their financial inhibitions.

Since rights and duties are two sides of the same coin, citizens may fulfil their legal obligations better if they can read and understand that their rights are 'subject to the respect for the rights and freedoms of others' (Article 12(2)). Besides, they will understand that their right to freedom is not absolute but subject to public interest (Article 12 (2)). Hence, any conduct or action, which violates public interest is subject to prosecution and the punishment related to the offence appropriately administered.

Additionally, the presumption of equality in the preamble, which is based on the social contract theory may not be realised if the citizens cannot read personally and understand what to do when they are arrested. They may not be aware that in the event that they are 'arrested, restricted or detained' they 'shall be informed immediately; in a language' which they understand and should be given 'the reasons for the arrest, restriction or detention' (Article 14 (2)). A citizen must also be aware that he or she has the right to engage the services of a lawyer of his or her choice as provided for in Article 14 (2). Generally, citizens must be aware of the protection of their personal liberty under the law (Article 14), the protection of their human dignity (Article 15) , the right to be accorded fair trial at a court (Article 19) as well as all other provisions in the Constitution that affect their rights must be known to them. In the absence of this knowledge where some citizens are not literate in English and cannot have access to the Constitution in a language they can read and understand, the rule of law as a pillar of democracy may become a mirage.

A person who is 'arrested, restricted or detained is expected to be arraigned before a court within forty–eight hours' (Article 14 (3b). However, there have been instances where some citizens of Ghana were arrested and detained but unfortunately they did not go through trial and remained in detention longer than usual. For instance, Tando (2017) writing for the Ghana News Agency reports how some 'accused persons had been in prison custody from five months to four years for various crimes, including murder, rape, stealing, and illegal possession of narcotic substances' (Tando, 2017, paragraph 1). According to Tando's (2017) report, these were 'eight remand prisoners at the Akuse Local Prison in the Eastern Region' who 'have been discharged, after two Courts sat on their cases, under the Justice for All Programme' (ibid). Possibly, if these affected citizens had read and known their rights, they may immediately, per Article 14 (2) of the Constitution, 1992, have solicited legal assistance from a lawyer of their choice. Granting that they are able to utilise this provision in the law, the appropriate remedies may be provided by the High Court 'in the nature of *habeas corpus, certiorari, mandamus*, prohibition, and *quo warranto* as it may consider appropriate for the purpose of enforcing or securing the enforcement of any of the provisions on the fundamental human rights and freedoms to the protection of which the person concerned is entitled' (Article 33 (2), 1992 Constitution).

Decolonising ourselves from the sanctimonious use of the English language after sixty years of independence and giving firm grounding to many Ghanaian languages as languages of literacy will be a remarkable stride towards democracy and the rule of law. As Ali Mazrui (1979, p.4) has observed, 'the very identity of African Countries is partly tied up with whether they speak English, French, Portuguese or some other imperial language.' After several years of independence, Ghana has to take a bold step to invest considerably in the teaching and learning of Ghanaian languages. This will make it possible for those who may not be able to read and write in English to read and write in at least one Ghanaian language.

Though successive governments in Ghana have tried to improve upon education and literacy in Ghana, the literacy rate in the country is not encouraging. The Ghana Living Standard Survey, Round 6 defines literacy as 'the ability to read and write simple sentences in English and any Ghanaian language with understanding' (Ghana Statistical Survey, 2014, p.17). According to the survey report, about 56.3% of Ghanaians who are 15 years and above can read and write in English. This implies that only a little over half of the population can read and write in English. Hence, 47.3 % of the population cannot access any written information in English intended to be circulated among citizens. This is why the translation of the Constitution and other statutes into Ghanaian languages is crucial.

Furthermore, whereas in the capital, Accra and other urban towns 69.6% of the population who are 15 years and above are literate in English, only 41.7% of the population can read and write in English in the rural areas. The report further shows that 35.7% of the adult population is literate in English language only whereas 28.4% are literate in a Ghanaian language only with only 11.7% being literate in both English and a Ghanaian language. The literacy rate paints a gloomy scenario for the development of democracy and the rule of law. In that, the constitution and other coded laws are alien to a considerable percentage of the population who cannot read and write in English. The total population of those who can read in a Ghanaian language is 40.1%. This includes those who can read and write in English and a Ghanaian language (11.7%) and those who can read and write in only a Ghanaian language (28.4%).

Such a massive population of less literate people, as noted above, may become straws that are easily blown by the wind of influence because they cannot read and understand things for themselves. Yet curiously, they may be living in the false hope that they believe in themselves and know everything. Mere belief and bravado without knowledge may produce the perpetuation of ignorance, abuse of law and attendant national retrogression. The laws then become what one may describe as legal effigies to which the majority of the populace cannot relate because they do not communicate to them.

Real development 'starts not with goods but with people, for unless people are educated, organised and principled, human resources will remain untapped and civilisation will be dwarfed' (Eboh, 1998, p. 139). This implies that people who cannot read the Constitution cannot obtain any education from the Constitution or any statute to guide their conduct to make them organised and principled because they cannot read about their basic rights and duties.

In an organised society, descriptive norms specify acceptable conduct while injunctive norms specify what is predominantly acceptable in a society (Severin & Tankard, 2001). The descriptive and injunctive norms in the Constitution and other statutes may not be obeyed to the letter since the populace cannot read them. Again, Gyekye (2004, p.39) has observed that, 'to be developed is to have the capacity to perform satisfactorily the functions appropriate to the object (*any living thing, whether human or non human*)'. Thus, though Chapter Five of the Constitution, 1995 provides for Fundamental Rights and Freedoms, if citizens neither have the capacity to perform their civic duties satisfactorily nor enjoy their rights fully, then there is a problem with development. A case in point is *Herman V Coffie* [1997-98]. In this Supreme Court case, it was held that the arrest by the police of the plaintiff's son when looking for the plaintiff was an action against the fundamental right of the plaintiff's son. Such cases may abound when people do not know their rights.

Also, either simultaneously or after the Constitution has been translated, the Criminal Code (Act 29) must be translated into as many Ghanaian languages as possible. For, 'a community of men and women who are intrinsically excellent will make better efforts than one composed of people who are ignorant and malevolent' (Eboh, 1998, p. 142).

## Conclusion

The inability of a considerable proportion of the Ghanaian population to read in English is a hindrance to the development of democracy and general advancement of the nation. More so, since there are no copies of the Constitution available in Ghanaian languages, many citizens may be groping in darkness as far as constitutional rights and responsibilities are concerned.

In translating the constitution and other laws into Ghanaian languages, the work must aim at communicating to the people through simple and direct language. Here, the mark of good language use by the lawyer and the judge must apply (Higgins & Tatham, 2011; Brobbey 2011). Again, as a post- colonial initiative, the translation of the Constitution and other laws must aim at decolonising the law not in terms of watering down the time- tested tradition of legal language but to make the law accessible to the ordinary citizen in a language he or she appreciates.

It is acknowledged that legal language is replete with poetry and literary devices (Schane, 2006; Tiersma, 1999). Schane (2006, p.5) for instance has observed that 'both specialised vocabulary and unusual sentence structure contribute to the peculiarities of legal writing.' These linguistic characteristics, which distinguish legal language can be vividly captured in local languages if teams of experts in Ghanaian languages and legal persons are engaged in the translation process. Ghana Institute of Linguistics, Literacy and Bible Translation (GILBT), Ghana Legal Council and other stakeholders must collaborate for the success of the agenda to translate the Constitution and other statutes into Ghanaian languages.

# 9

# LEGISLATING SUSTAINABLE DEVELOPMENT: GHANA'S PATH TO DEVELOPMENT

## Edmund Ato Kwaw
## P. Ebow Bondzi-Simpson

**Abstract**

Most countries agree, notwithstanding definitional difficulties, that achieving sustainable development is a worthwhile objective. However, making verbal commitments is one thing, and translating such verbal commitments into practice, is quite another. Governmental decision-making in Ghana has, on the whole, and for a variety of reasons, been unable to move from mere verbal commitments to concrete efforts. On June 3, 2015, Accra, the capital of Ghana, witnessed massive flooding, resulting in loss of life and property. All agree that the flooding was the result of decades of unsustainable development. Recent exposés regarding the rampant destruction of arable and riparian resources in Ghana from illegal small-scale mining (galamsey) activities is also evidence of the enduring inability to translate verbal commitments regarding sustainable development, into concrete efforts.

After 60 years of independence, has the time come to use force; to legislate change in the direction of sustainable development? The paper argues that the answer is a resounding yes. While passivity concerning the implementation of sustainable development may not be crucial for other countries' developments, it is crucial for the growth of the developing countries in Africa such as Ghana.

Thus, legislation has a critical role to play and Ghana's legislature must take a proactive role in advancing sustainable development through the enactment of a viable legal framework for the implementation of sustainable development. The sustainable development legislation of several jurisdictions, including Canada, and the Province of Quebec in Canada, and Malta, provide excellent examples of how to devise the appropriate legislation for the implementation of sustainable development in Ghana.

## Introduction

Most agree, notwithstanding definitional difficulties, that sustainable development is the key to development in Africa. The three dimensions of sustainable development, namely inclusive social development, inclusive economic development, and sustainable environment, cut across all sectors of development, embracing matters such as urbanization, agriculture, infrastructure, energy development and use, land use, sanitation, water availability, transportation, health, equality and democratic governance. For most countries then, achieving sustainable development is a worthwhile objective and the issue is not whether to embrace sustainable development, but how to translate verbal commitments concerning sustainable development into reality. Ever since the United Nations Conference on Environment and Development held in Rio de Janeiro, Brazil in 1992 (the Earth Summit), Ghana and countries on the continent have made significant efforts to pursue and achieve sustainable development. Sadly, however, sustainable development has remained elusive.

How can Ghana translate its commitments respecting sustainable development into reality? This paper argues that the time has come for Ghana to use force; to legislate sustainable development. Legislation makes possible the adoption and enforcement of an integrated approach to development, taking into consideration economic, social and environmental matters, that will set the country on a reliable path to development.

Indeed, Agenda 21 of the Earth Summit, which was adopted by more than 178 countries, makes it clear that to achieve sustainable development all countries must build up and implement integrated, sanction-obliging and effective laws and regulations that comply with well conceived social, ecological, economic and scientific principles.[1]

1 *United Nations Conference on Environment & Development; Agenda 21*, held in Rio de Janerio, Brazil, 3 to 14 June 1992. Available at https://sustainabledevelopment.un.org/content/documents/Agenda21.pdf.

The paper commences with a brief discussion of the concept of sustainable development, the history of its evolution, the three dimensions of sustainable development and why achieving sustainable development is important for the development of Ghana. It then proceeds to discuss some of the strategies that Ghana has pursued in the bid to achieve sustainable development and why these strategies have failed. The paper follows that with a discussion of the role that legislation can play in the successful implementation of sustainable development. Finally, adopting a comparative approach, it draws on examples from countries that have passed sustainable development legislation and suggests model provisions of a sustainable development law for the country.

## I. Historical Background and Definition of Sustainable Development

Though concern for the environment has been a constant concern throughout human history, and the roots of the notion of sustainability can be traced to ancient times,[2] the origin of the concept of sustainable development can be traced to a new mode of thinking about the link between development and the environment that emerged in the late 1960s and early 1970s, challenging erstwhile thinking about 'progress,' 'unlimited economic growth,' and development.[3] Prior to this period it had been assumed that the problems of development that plagued the developing world could be resolved primarily through world-wide economic growth.

While the term 'sustainable development' is said to have been coined in the 1970s[4] by Barbara Ward, the founder of the International Institute for Environment and Development, the current conceptual underpinning of the notion of sustainable development owes its origins to a number of other sources.

The first of these is the report of the Club of Rome, titled *The Limits of Growth*,[5] which warned of an impending catastrophe because of global over-consumption of the earth's finite natural resources, and set the stage for a more focussed discussion of alternatives to unbridled economic growth.[6] The

2 Jacobus Du Pisani "Sustainable Development – Historical Roots of the Concept" (2006) 3 *Environmental Sciences* 83.

3 ibid 89

4 See B. Ward and R. Dubos *Only one earth – The care and maintenance of a small plant* (Deutsch 1972).

5 Donella Meadows, Dennis Meadows and William Behrens III *Limits to growth* (New American Library 1972).

6 Du Pisani (n) 2, 90.

publication also brought about a paradigm shift in development dialogue to a new notion of development; one that embraced the idea of development as well as conservation. The *Limits of Growth* called for an order of ecological and economic stability that could be sustained far into the future, and was capable of meeting the needs of all people.

The Club of Rome Report was followed by a series of international conferences on the threatening ecological crisis, which further clarified the concept of sustainable development.

The first of these was the United Nations Conference on Human Environment which took place in Stockholm in 1972. This conference, which was the first major international recognition of the concept of sustainable development, was also the first international assessment of the global human impact on the environment. On June 16, 1972, the conference adopted the *Declaration of the United Nations Conference on the Human Environment*,[7] which proclaimed among other things, that

> "1. Man is both a creature and moulder of his environment, which gives him physical sustenance and affords him the opportunity for intellectual, moral, social, and spiritual growth. In the long and tortuous evolution of the human race on this planet a stage has been reached when, through the rapid acceleration of science and technology, man has acquired the power to transform his environment in countless ways and on an unprecedented scale. Both aspects of man's environment, the natural and the man-made, are essential to his well-being and to the enjoyment of basic human rights the right to life itself.
> 2. The protection and improvement of the human environment is a major issue which affects the well-being of peoples and economic development throughout the world; it is the urgent desire of the peoples of the whole world and the duty of all Governments."

With this Declaration, the conference raised global awareness of environmental concerns that had hitherto been little discussed, and agreed that the prevailing dichotomy in development practise between development, on the one hand, and the environment, on the other, no longer made sense.

---

7 Also known as the Stockholm Declaration; adopted, June 16, 1972; U.N. Doc. A/Conf.48/14Rev. 1. Reprinted in 11 ILM (1972) 1416.

Both development and environment had to be managed efficiently for mutual benefit.

By the 1980s the concept of sustainable development had become popular and was being more widely used. For instance, the International Union for the Conservation of Natural Resources (IUCN) used the expression in their publication *World Conservation Strategy*.[8] In the publication, they argued that conservation of nature and development were inextricably linked, and that conservation cannot be achieved without efforts to alleviate poverty and the misery of the world's millions.

A major boost to the concept came in 1987, when the 22 person World Commission on Environment and Development (the Brundtland Commission) set up in 1983,[9] and tasked by the United Nations to formulate a global agenda for change respecting environment and development, presented its report.[10] In its Report, titled Our common future, the Brundtland Commission focused chiefly on human needs and interests, and declared that the time had come for a permanent link to be established between the environment and the economy. It defined sustainable development as "development that meets the needs of the present, without compromising the ability of future generations to meet their own needs."[11] Further, it linked social, economic, cultural and environmental issues, and global solutions, and expressed the belief that social equity, economic growth and environmental maintenance were not mutually exclusive dimensions of development, but went hand-in-hand.

The next important world gathering on sustainable development took place in 1992 in Rio de Janeiro, Brazil, (the Earth Summit), leading to the adoption of the Rio Declaration on Environment and Development, and Agenda 21. These documents spelt out the principles and action plan for sustainable development respectively. The first four principles of the Rio Declaration justify sustainable development, thusly.

8 World Conservation Strategy, (International Union for the Conservation of Natural Resources, 1980).

9 The Brundtland Commission was named after Gro Harlem Brundtland, the former Prime minister of Norway who was the Chair of the Commission.

10 *Our common future*, Report of the World Commission on Environment and Development, (Oxford University Press 1987).

11 ibid.

**Principle 1**

Human beings are at the centre of concerns for sustainable development. They are entitled to a healthy and productive life in harmony with nature.

**Principle 2**

States have, in accordance with the Charter of the United Nations and the principles of international law, the sovereign right to exploit their own resources pursuant to their own environmental and developmental policies, and the responsibility to ensure that activities within their jurisdiction or control do not cause damage to the environment of other States or of areas beyond the limits of national jurisdiction.

**Principle 3**

The right to development must be fulfilled so as to equitably meet developmental and environmental needs of present and future generations.

**Principle 4**

In order to achieve sustainable development, environmental protection shall constitute an integral part of the development process and cannot be considered in isolation from it.

Following on the Rio summit, other international conferences concerning sustainable development have also been convened. These include the *International Conference on Population and Development (ICPD), Cairo, Egypt, 1994*, which dealt with issues concerning reproductive health, sustained economic growth, poverty eradication, and empowerment of women and girls; the *Fourth World Conference on Women, Beijing, China, 1995*, which came out with the Beijing Declaration and Platform for Action that endorsed several of the sustainable development goals identified at the Rio Summit; the Millennium Summit of September 8, 2000, which resulted in the adoption by the General Assembly of the United Nations of the Millennium Declaration and eight Millennium Development Goals (MDGs); the *World Summit on Sustainable Development, Johannesburg, South Africa, 2002*, which turned out the Johannesburg Declaration on Sustainable Development, whose primary focus was the persistent "worldwide conditions that pose threats to sustainable development," including chronic hunger, malnutrition, armed conflict, intolerance and incitement to racial, ethnic, religious and other hatreds, and endemic, communicable and chronic diseases, in particular HIV/AIDS, malaria and tuberculosis; and the June 2012, United Nations Conference on Sustainable Development (UNCSD), also known as Rio 2012 or Rio+20 Summit.

Following the adoption of the Millennium Development Goals, there was broad criticism that the eight goals were two narrow. Among other criticisms, it was conceded that there was the need to consider the root causes of poverty, which the MDGs failed to do. It was further argued that it disregarded gender inequalities as well as the all encompassing nature of development. Critics also indicated that it ignored the importance of the promotion of human rights to poverty alleviation, and made no direct reference to economic development as an engine of poverty alleviation. It was also acknowledged that while the MDGs were supposed to apply to all countries, they were, in reality, intended to provide a focal point for poor country policies. This one-sided approach to global poverty alleviation, it was agreed, would not work. There was thus the need for a new all embracing agenda that would build on the MDGs.

At the Rio+20 Summit, then, member states adopted a resolution[12] committing to initiate a process to develop a set of Sustainable Development Goals (SDGs) that would build upon the MDGs. Then, in September 25, 2015, the 193 countries of the UN General Assembly adopted the 2030 Development Agenda titled *Transforming our world: the 2030 Agenda for Sustainable Development* or Agenda 2030, setting out a plan over the next 15 years to end extreme poverty, fight inequality and injustice, and protect the planet. Paragraph 51 of the 92 paragraph document outlined the 17 Sustainable Development Goals (SDGs)[13] and the associated 169 targets. The seventeen goals are as follows:

> Goal 1: Eliminate all forms of poverty everywhere
> Goal 2: End hunger and the causes of hunger, and promote sustainable agricultural practices
> Goal 3: Ensure good health and well-being for all, at all ages
> Goal 4: Ensure quality education for all
> Goal 5: Achieve gender equality and the empowerment of women and girls.
> Goal 6: Ensure access to clean water and sanitation for all.
> Goal 7: Provide access to affordable and clean energy for all.

12 UN Resolution A/RES/66/288.
13 UN Resolution A/RES/70/1

Goal 8: Advance inclusive and sustainable economic growth and ensure productive employment and decent work for all

Goal 9: Create durable infrastructure, promote innovation, and ensure sustainable industrialization

Goal 10: Reduce all forms of inequality within and among countries

Goal 11: Promote and ensure safe, resilient and sustainable cities and communities

Goal 12: Ensure responsible consumption and production practices

Goal 13: Combat climate change and the impact of climate change

Goal 14: Ensure sustainable use of ocean and marine resources

Goal 15: Protect and ensure the sustainable use of the earth's resources

Goal 16: Promote peaceful and inclusive societies with strong institutions, and guarantee the rule of law

Goal 17: Create and revitalise partnerships to implement and achieve the SDGs for sustainable development.

Briefly, then, sustainable development "focuses on meeting peoples' social and economic needs within natural resource limits, so that human development can be both sustainable and sustained."[14]

## A. Dimensions of Sustainable Development

There are three dimensions of sustainable development, namely (a) inclusive social development, (b) inclusive economic development, and (c) sustainable environment.

## (i) Inclusive Development

Inclusive development, comprising the twin notions of inclusive social development and inclusive economic development is founded on two concepts: inclusion, and development. Inclusion is a process as well as a goal. While diversity is a fact of life, the tragedy is that many persons are excluded from society because of their differences, including gender, ethnicity, age, disability and poverty. Inclusion involves making society more accommodating, and combating discrimination of all kinds.

14 *Sustainable Development Starts and Ends with Safe, Healthy and Well-Educated Children*, (UNICEF 2013).

Development has been defined in many ways and a detailed discussion of these myriad definitions far exceeds the scope of this paper. Briefly, it may be defined as the development of the economic wealth of countries or regions for the well-being of their inhabitants. Development thus encompasses far more than economic growth and is distinguished from it. It involves a progressive change in the socio-economic structure of nations. While economic growth is the mere measure of a rise in output, development is a

> "comprehensive economic, social, cultural and political process, which aims at the constant improvement of the well-being of the entire population and of all individuals."[15]

Comparatively then, economic growth is easier to achieve than development. Economic growth requires a larger mobilisation of resources and the raising of productivity, but development requires more than a mere rise in output. It involves changes in the composition of output, shifts in the allocation of productive resources, and elimination and/or reduction of poverty, inequalities and unemployment. As Amartya Sen notes,

> "Development requires the removal of major sources of unfreedom, poverty as well as tyranny, poor economic opportunities, as well as social deprivation, neglect of public facilities, as well as intolerance or over activity or repressive states…"[16]

The key components of development are (a) poverty alleviation, (b) human rights, and (c) civil society participation. Under the Millennium Development Goals (MDGs), countries committed themselves to achieving eight measurable goals, by mobilising efforts to end all forms of poverty, fighting inequalities, and tackling climate change. The MDGs, which were intended to provide a framework around which developmental policies could be fashioned, provided a basic framework for inclusive development which continue to be relevant. These are the:

- eradication of extreme poverty and hunger
- achievement of universal primary education

15 Christina Gille and Stefanie Ricarda Roos (2001) *German Law Journal* reprinted at http:www. german lawjournal.com/article.php?id=131. See also *Declaration on the Right to Development*, UN Res. 41/128, December 4, 1986.
16 Amartya Sen *Freedom as Development* (Oxford University Press 1999).

- promotion of gender equality and empowerment of women
- reduction in child mortality
- improvement in maternal health, and
- promotion of environmental sustainability

Inclusive Development is thus the process of ensuring that all marginalised or excluded groups are included in the process of social and economic development.

## (ii) Sustainable Environment

Environmental sustainability was one of the key components of the MDGs and is foundered on the principle that everything needed for human survival and well-being depends, either directly or indirectly, on the environment. Environmental sustainability involves creating and maintaining the conditions under which humans and nature can exist in productive harmony, so that the social, economic and other requirements of present and future generations can be fulfilled.

As aptly explained by a UNICEF document, the interrelationship between inclusive social development, inclusive economic development and sustainable environment involves "the continued advance of poverty eradication, human rights, and equity, while also realising more sustainable patterns of human consumption and production, stabilising climatic forces and sustainably managing our common natural resource base."[17]

Currently, sustainable development is viewed as a central concept in the area of international development law, embracing notions of poverty eradication, environmental protection, governance and economic development.

## II. The Pursuit and Implementation of Sustainable Development in Ghana

The upshot of the above conferences and summits on sustainable development was to strengthen individual country and global commitments towards the pursuit of, and achievement of sustainable development. There is consensus that achieving sustainable development is a valuable objective and that sustainable development holds the key to lifting African countries like

---

17 *Sustainable Development Starts and Ends with Safe, Healthy and Well-Educated Children,* (UNICEF 2013) 4.

Ghana out of poverty, and setting them on the path to development. Members of the global community are required to develop and implement country-specific strategies—taking into consideration the shared issues identified by the international community—to pursue and achieve the objectives of sustainable development.

Over the past few decades, Ghana and other African countries have renewed their commitments and efforts, individually, as well as jointly, to implement sustainable development. Jointly, these efforts include the establishment of the *New Partnership for Development* (NEPAD) in 2001, to provide a common vision, and collaborative means of eradicating poverty on the continent; the *Gaborone Declaration of Sustainability in Africa*, the result of a two day summit on sustainability by ten African heads of state and public and private partners in May 2012, where African countries recommitted themselves to pursuing sustainable development by implementing all conventions on the subject; and the adoption of the *Cairo Declaration on Managing Africa's Natural Capital for Sustainable Development and Poverty Eradication* by African ministers of the environment at the African Ministerial Conference on the Environment on March 6, 2015.

## A. Ghana's Action Plans and Strategies to Achieve Sustainable Development

Individually, countries on the continent have instituted a combination of plans and strategies, and enacted sector specific legislation with a view to implementing sustainable development. Ghana's efforts are one such example.

In Ghana, until 2011, there was no clear policy respecting the pursuit of sustainable development. What prevailed were a series of national development strategies that indirectly impacted the pursuit of sustainable development. These include the Ghana Poverty Reduction Strategy (GPRS I), which was implemented from 2003 to 2005; and the Growth and Poverty Reduction Strategy (GPRS II), which was implemented from 2006 to 2009.

Other sector specific strategic and action plans, programs, and national and institutional development plans, of a general nature, that have or are being pursued with the object of fulfilling Ghana's commitment to achieving the Rio Declaration and Agenda 21 objectives, include the following: *Ghana Shared Growth and Development Agenda* I and II (GSGDA I): 2010-2013 and (GSGDA II): 2014-2017, both medium term plans that concern the transformation of the economy through industrialisation, and the sustainable exploration of resources, among others; *National Social Protection Strategy* (NSPS): 2007, which started several social protection programs, including the *Livelihood Economic Advancement Program* (LEAP), which initiated a program of social cash transfers and free health insurance for vulnerable people; *National Environmental Sanitation Strategy and Action Plan* (NESSAP): 2010, which reaffirmed the importance of environmental sanitation, and provided strategies to guide Metropolitan, Municipal, and District Assemblies; *National Health Insurance Scheme* (NHIS), which introduced a contribution scheme for health insurance in 2003; *National Climate Change Policy, 2013*, which outlined the government's approach and response to the challenges of climate change; *Ghana School Feeding Program* (GSFP), which introduced the one hot meal a day for every school child in 2003; *Food and Agricultural Sector Development Plans* (FASDEP) I and II, in 2002 & 2007, concerning, respectively, the implementation of strategies for (i) modernising the agricultural sector and (ii) the sustainable utilisation of resources; *Medium Term Agriculture Sector Investment Plan* (METASIP), 2009-2015, which is the investment plan that is intended to implement the medium term programmes of FASDEP I&II; *Forest Investment Plan* (FIP) of 2012, which is intended to address the causes of deforestation and invest in strategies to reduce emissions from deforestation and forest degradation (REDD).

In 2011, the government of Ghana came up with the *Sustainable Development Action Plan* (SDAP), 2011-2016, also referred to as the National Programme on Sustainable Consumption and Production (SCP). In June 2012, it unveiled the *Sustainable Energy for All Action Plan*, (SE4ALL), which was the government's response to the call by the United Nations for all Member States to increase awareness of energy issues and promote the sustainable use of energy resources.

## B. Statutory Expressions of Sustainable Development

In addition to the above, the pursuit of sustainable development in Ghana has also found expression in a number of legislation, including the (a) Social Security Act, 1965; (b) Social Security Law, 1991; (c) Children's Act, 1998; (d) the Intestate Succession Law, and (e) Juvenile Justice Act, to name a few.

## C. Challenges to the Attainment of Sustainable Development

Despite the adoption of these strategic plans, the enactment of the above statutes, and the development of a sustainable development policy, the attainment of sustainable development has remained elusive for Ghana.

A report sponsored by UNICEF, the Ghana Poverty and Inequality Report[18], shows that as at 2016, one out of four persons in Ghana lived in poverty and inequality was at its highest level since 2005.

Child poverty also continues to be a problem in Ghana, with three out of every ten children living in poverty, and one out of this three living in extreme poverty.[19] Further, a Ghanaian child is 40% more likely to live in poverty than an adult.[20] Given the nature of the poverty vicious cycle, this means three out of every ten children—in real terms, 3.65 million children as of 2012/13[21]— will grow up to be poor adults, plagued by health problems, malnutrition, and with very little ability to contribute to national development.

Environmental problems also continue to plague the country. For instance, Accra, the country's capital has experienced severe floods, leading to outbreaks of cholera, and other waterborne diseases during the rainy season for many decades, including in June 1959; on July 4, 1968; July 5, 1995; June 13, 1997; June 28, 2001; May 5, 2010; February 24, 2011; November 1, 2011; May 31, 2013; June 6, 2014; July 4, 2014; June 3, 2015; December 10, 2017; and as recently as February 13, 2018.[22] To date, apart from dredging rivers and cleaning out drains, no specific sustainable strategy has been crafted to deal

18 Edgar Cooke, Sarah Hague and Andy MacKay, *The Ghana Poverty and Inequality Report-2016* (UNICEF 2016)

19 *Child Poverty* (UNICEF 2015), hereinafter *Child Poverty*. See also Edgar Cooke, Sarah Hague and Andy MacKay, *Ghana Poverty and Inequality Report* (n) 18, 1.

20 Edgar Cooke, Sarah Hague, & Andy MacKay, *Ghana Poverty and Inequality Report*, 2.

21 *Child Poverty* (n) 19, 1.

22 For accounts of the flood, see David Smith, "Death toll rises in Accra floods and petrol station fire," in *The Guardian Online*, Friday, 5, June , 2015, at https://www.theguardian.com/world/2015/ jun/05/death-toll-accra-floods-petrol-station-fire, (accessed on 6, May 2018); "Photos: Floods, fire disaster kill hundred plus in Accra," at https://www.myjoyonline.com/news/2015/june-4th/ photosfloods-fire-disaster-kill-hundred-plus-in-accra.php, (accessed on 5, May, 2018); and Ghana National Fire Service, "June 3rd disaster," at http://gnfs.gov.gh/article/june-3rd-disaster, (accessed on 6, May, 2018).

with this annual occurrence. Observers agree that this annual flooding is the result of decades of unsustainable development.[23]

Since the early part of this year too, news reporting in Ghana has been inundated with exposés regarding the rampant destruction of arable and riparian resources from illegal small scale mining, or 'galamsey', activities, notwithstanding the existence of the country's Sustainable Development Action Plan (SDAP), 2011-2016, and the Ghana Shared Growth and Development Agenda I and II (GSGDA I), 2010-2013 and (GSGDA II): 2014-2017.

Why has the adoption of these plans, and the enactment of the mentioned laws not resulted in the attainment of sustainable development? It is true that Ghana has encountered challenges such as poverty, the mismanagement of public resources, and rampant corruption, all of which hamper the achievement of sustainable development. However, the above challenges are just that; challenges, and not the cause of the failure of the strategic plans to bring about sustainable development. Indeed, sustainable development initiatives are intended to resolve these challenges. The primary reason for the failure of Ghana and the other countries on the continent to achieve sustainable development, despite the adoption of strategies and action plans, is twofold. The first is the deficiencies in the plans themselves, and the second is the absence of a legislative foundation for sustainable development.

## 1. Deficiencies in the Strategic Plans

There are two categories of deficiencies in the strategic and action plans: inherent deficiencies, and implementation deficiencies.

## (a) Inherent Deficiencies

Inherent deficiencies are deficiencies that are inbuilt in the nature of a process; in this case the action or strategic plan. Briefly, while the creation of sustainable development plans is evidence of a commitment on the part

23 See for instance, Samuel Asumadu-Sarkodie, Phebe Asantewa Owusu & Patrick Rufangura "Impact analysis of flood in Accra," (2015) 6(9) *Advances in Applied Science Research* 53-78; Available online at http://www.pelagiaresearchlibrary.com/. Seth J. Bokpe "Annual floods in Accra, an engineering failure," *Daily Graphic*, 10, June, 2015, available on line at https://www.graphic.com.gh/news/general-news/annual-floods-in-accra-an-engineering-failure.html+&cd=3&hl=en&ct=clnk&gl=gh (accessed on 6, May, 2018).

of the government, these plans, be they characterised as strategic or action plans, are just that, plans. Such is the nature of the numerous plans adopted in Ghana. They are merely intended courses of action—some of which spell out in detail the proposed courses of action—and impose no obligation on the part of either the planner, or the recipients of the plans to carry it out. There is thus no compulsion on those on whom has been placed the task to implement the plan to do so, and there is no ability to enforce their conduct, or impose sanctions. Typically, the election of a political party in power has also meant the elimination of all plans initiated by that party. Hence, the plans, by their very nature, have been ineffective methods of implementing sustainable development.

### (b) Implementation Deficiencies

Implementation deficiencies in the strategic plans are also a major reason for the failure to achieve sustainable development. Implementation deficiencies include (i) the absence of a single oversight body, (ii) fractionalization of planning and implementation, (iii) lack of expertise, and (iv) the absence of conditions of accountability.

### (i) The Absence of a Single Oversight Body

Sustainable development is not confined to a single subject matter, and cuts across several disciplines. This means that its implementation is not restricted to a single governmental authority or sector ministry. The successful carrying out of any efforts aimed at attaining sustainable development thus requires an approach that integrates multiple administrative efforts aimed at realising the three dimensions of sustainable development. This necessarily requires a single entity that has the expertise (or is able to obtain the expertise), and is able and authorized to coordinate the planning and implementation of sustainable development. Indeed, Agenda 21 recommends that countries establish single bodies called National Commissions or Councils on sustainable development in order to ensure the effective implementation of sustainable development agreements.

In Ghana, there is no single entity that is given this mandate. Currently, there are several governmental organizations that are, in theory, involved in formulating and implementing sustainable development strategies in Ghana. These include, the National Development Planning Commission (NDPC);

Ministry of the Environment Science, Technology and Innovation (MESTI); and Environmental Protection Agency (EPA).

The EPA is the main body that is directly responsible for matters concerning environmental management and protection, and formulating policies and strategies respecting the environment. The NDPC oversees the preparation, coordination, implementation and monitoring of medium-term strategic plans, including sustainable development plans, prepared by the Metropolitan, Municipal and District Assemblies (MMDAs), and the Ministries, Departments and Agencies (MDAs). The MESTI is responsible for formulating policy issues, and also oversees the work of six statutory bodies that are concerned in one way or another with sustainable development. These statutory bodies are the EPA, Town and Country Planning Department, Council for Scientific and Industrial Research, Ghana Atomic Energy Commission, Rural Enterprises Project and the Environmental Resources Management Project.

Under Ghana's SDAP also, a multi-stakeholder sustainable development committee oversees the implementation of the SDAP. This committee comprises the Environmental Protection Agency, the National Development Planning Commission, Ghana Statistical Service, Ghana Chamber of Mines, Ghana Chamber of Commerce and Industry, Water Resources Commission, Forestry Commission, Energy Commission, and Minerals Commission.

This multiplicity of bodies with overlapping mandates when it comes to implementing sustainable development—a 'too many cooks syndrome'—leads to poor implementation of programs and projects concerning sustainable development. The environmental degradation caused by the illegal small scale mining or 'galamsey' scourge in the country, is a clear example of what happens when there is no single oversight body. Before the media started reporting on the environmental degradation being caused by illegal small scale mining activities, no entity in the country seemed to be responsible for ensuring that small scale mining activities were undertaken in a sustainable manner. Though small-scale mining falls under the purview of the Ministry of Lands and Natural Resources of Ghana, the ministry was given no clear role in enforcing sustainable development practices regarding small-scale mining activities. Indeed, the Small-scale Gold Mining Law, 1989 (PNDCL 218) says nothing about sustainable development.

Further, given its name, one would have thought that the responsibility for ensuring the implementation of sustainable development practices in small-scale mining in Ghana would fall on the shoulders of the Environmental

Protection Agency of Ghana. Indeed, the website of the Agency states that "the Environmental Protection Agency is the leading public body for protecting and improving the environment in Ghana." In practice, however, the role of the EPA, as the website also touts, is limited to advising the sector ministry "on the formulation of policies on all aspects of the environment and in particular making recommendations for the protection of the environment." Accordingly, it does not have a sustainable development audit function or role, which would empower it to audit sustainable development activities of different institutions, whether public or private, and if appropriate, require that they undertake remedial action.

### (ii) Fractionalization of Planning and Implementation

A further implementation deficiency is the fractionalization of the planning and implementation processes. Since sustainable development is a national commitment, necessarily, the approach to its planning, pursuit and implementation must be national, this means that it must engage the national government, and there must be a national implementation plan. This is crucial even in the case of federal jurisdictions, or where, as in the case of Ghana, a system of decentralized planning is practiced.

In Ghana, however, while there are national 'action' plans, and national 'strategic' plans, there is no national implementation plan. Indeed, local governments in Ghana are required to prepare and submit their own plans for implementing sustainable development in their respective areas. Where there are national divisions, or, as in the case of Ghana, a system of decentralized planning exists, and the units are required to prepare their own plans, a free-for-all is the likely result, with little, if any, reference to any rules or policies underpinning an overall national strategy. This severely impacts the attainment of sustainable development.

### (iii) Lack of Expertise

Where a decentralised system of planning exists, and the local planning units lack the required expertise to understand what sustainable development means, and its role in governance, any sustainable development plan which is dependent on such local authorities preparing their own plans, is bound to fail. This will hamper the achievement of sustainable development. This is the case with local authorities in Ghana. Research conducted by the authors indicates that while local governments are required to prepare and submit their sustainable development plans for their localities, none of the local authorities have on staff persons who have any training whatsoever in the area of sustainable development.

### (iv) Absence of Accountability Mechanisms

Accountability mechanisms ensure that government departments and authorities that are given responsibilities concerning the advancement of sustainable development, are held to their obligations and promises. Currently, under the various development plans and Ghana's SDAP, there is no system of accountability and there is no clear monitoring and evaluation process concerning the implementation of sustainable development. In the absence of accountability mechanisms, there is no compulsion on the part of any governmental department or local authority to do what it is either obliged, or has undertaken to do. This has hampered the attainment of sustainable development in the country.

### 2. The Absence of a Legislative Foundation for Sustainable Development

To bring about social change, the enactment of policy and plans is only the first step. Since law is the most powerful tool available to Governments to implement long-term policy and influence change, and is the major determinant of social transformation, legislation is the indispensable second step.[24]

---

24 An in-depth discussion of law and social change far exceeds the scope of this paper. The reader may consult the following other discussions on the subject, Roger Cotterrell *The Sociology of Law*, (Oxford University Press 2007); Judy Fudge "What Do We Mean by Law and Social Transformation?" (1990) 5 *Canadian Journal of Law and Society* 47-70; S. Brickey and E. Comack, "The Role of Law in Social Transformation: Is a Jurisprudence of Insurgency Possible?" (1987) 2 *Canadian Journal of Law and Society* 97; and A. Bartholemew and S. Boyd, "The Political Economy of Law," in Wallace Clement and Glen Williams (eds.), *The New Canadian Political Economy* (McGill Queen's University Press 1989) 212.

## III. Legislating Sustainable Development in Ghana

While the creation of a sustainable development plan is important because it sets the stage for the pursuit and eventual achievement of sustainable development, the best way to achieve the multidisciplinary integration of different ministries which the planning and execution of sustainable development plans requires, is through legislation.

### A. The Importance of Legislation to Sustainable Development

Legislation, as the term is often used, includes Acts of Parliament, regulations, by-laws and instruments made under those Acts. While legislation performs many functions in society,[25] its primary importance involves the administration of government, and it is crucial for the achievement of sustainable development for two reasons. First, it triggers and crystallises changes in consciousness, public policy and social values, and second, it codifies rights inherent or embedded in new social values.

### (1) Triggering and Crystallising Changes in Consciousness, Public Policy and Values

In practical terms, the objective of all legislation is to regulate behaviour by specifying acceptable and unacceptable conduct, for instance making it an offence to (i) make certain comments about women, (ii) kill another person, (iii) drive a vehicle without a license, and (iv) litter. In real terms, by specifying what is acceptable and unacceptable, legislation also changes attitudes about the conduct concerned; getting people to understand and accept the morality enshrined in the acceptable conduct.[26] Legislation becomes a source of moral guidance with the result that behavior and attitudes that would have been acceptable and deemed to be normal become repugnant. Essentially, then, the successful implementation of any government program or plan, including the societal recognition of the validity of such a program, especially programs that depend on and/or require attitudinal changes, hinges on legislation.

25 Ed. Rubin, "Law and legislation in the administrative state," (1989) 89 *Columbia L. Rev.* 369-426.
26 See Bilz Kenworthey and Janice Nadler, "Law, moral attitudes and behavioural change," in Eyal Zamir & Doron Teichman, (eds) *The Oxford Handbook of Behavioural Economics and the Law* (Oxford University Press 2014) 241

## 2. Codifying Rights Inherent or Embedded in New Social Values

For a country such as Ghana, legislation is also necessary for the successful implementation of sustainable development because legislation would enshrine sustainable development in the country's laws by

(1) giving legal backing to the policy of sustainable development,

(2) affording priority to sustainable development across different sectors of government,

(3) increasing support for sustainable development programs and initiatives across government,

(4) granting protection to and validating sustainable development projects across government, especially environmental initiatives, and

(5) enabling the creation of indicators for the measurement of sustainable development, and the establishment of tools for monitoring and evaluating such indicators.

Further, in Ghana as well as other countries on the continent, the partisan nature of politics gives rise to a tendency where a newly elected government rejects the plans and policies of the government it is succeeding, and then institutes its own. This subjects sustainable development plans to the vicissitudes of the democratic process. Giving legal backing to sustainable development plans through legislation, thus guarantees the continuity of the plan.

Ghana has reached the point where legislation is needed to drive the implementation of sustainable development. The time has come for Ghana to legislate sustainable development.

## B. Possible Legislative Options for Ghana – Crafting a Statute

What then is the nature of the legislation that is required? What form should it take? There are three models of sustainable development implementing legislation. These are (i) the procedural model, (ii) the model that establishes the sustainable development strategy, and (iii) the model that establishes the attainment of sustainable development as the central operating principle of governmental decision making.[27]

27 Andrea Ross "It's time to get serious – Why legislation is needed to make sustainable development a reality in the U.K.?" (2010) 2 *Sustainability* 1102, 1112-1113. See also John Dernbach and Joel Mintz, "Environmental laws and sustainability," (2011) 3 *Sustainability* 531, 538.

No single model is completely satisfactory. Drawing on examples from different jurisdictions, this paper tables the position that the most appropriate model for Ghana is one that blends the features of all three, and provides for the (1) statement of a purpose, (2) establishment of a process for the sustainable development plan, (3) statement of the plan's methodology, including areas of intervention, (4) identification of the entity or body that is responsible for implementing the strategy or plan, (5) statement of principles or overriding policy that will guide decision making, and (6) appropriate monitoring and enforcement procedures.

## (1) Statement of Purpose

A sustainable development statute must clearly indicate its purpose. *The Sustainable Development Act* of the Province of Quebec, in Canada,[28] is instructive in this regard. It provides as follows:

> "1. The object of this Act is to establish a new management framework within the Administration to ensure that powers and responsibilities are exercised in the pursuit of sustainable development.
>
> The measures introduced by this Act are intended, more specifically, to bring about the necessary change within society with respect to non-viable development methods by further integrating the pursuit of sustainable development into the policies, programs and actions of the Administration, at all levels and in all areas of intervention. They are designed to ensure that government actions in the area of sustainable development are coherent and to enhance the accountability of the Administration in that area, in particular through the controls exercised by the Sustainable Development Commissioner under the Auditor General Act."

Stating the purpose clarifies the intent of the legislation, ensures that successive governments are bound by this statement of purpose, and assists in interpretation if needed.

28 SQ, c. D-8.1.1

## (2) The Establishment of a Process for the Sustainable Development Plan

To give the process of establishing the sustainable development strategy the backing of law, the legislation must clearly set out a process for the establishment of the sustainable development plan or strategy, as opposed to setting out the strategy itself. Setting out the strategy itself in the legislation is inappropriate as it may make it difficult for the strategy to be periodically reviewed. The provision setting out the process could also specify the principle or principles on which the sustainable development strategy is to be established. An example of such a provision is the Canadian federal *Sustainable Development Act*,[29] which requires the federal government to create and implement a government-wide sustainable development strategy in accordance with the precautionary principle, as follows,

> "9. (1) Within two years after this Act comes into force and within every three-year period after that, the Minister shall develop, in accordance with this section, a Federal Sustainable Development Strategy based on the precautionary principle."

## (3) Statement of Goals Targets, Areas of Intervention of the Strategic Plan

While it would be imprudent for the sustainable development legislation to contain details of the strategy itself, it is essential for the effectiveness and legal validity of the strategy, that the legislation specify the nuts and bolts of the strategy, or what should go into the strategy, including goals, targets, and areas of intervention. An example of such a provision is in the Canadian federal *Sustainable Development Act*, which provides in this regard as follows:

> "9.(2) The Federal Sustainable Development Strategy shall set out federal sustainable development goals and targets and an implementation strategy for meeting each target and identify the minister responsible for meeting each target...
> 11. (1) Each Minister presiding over a department named in Schedule I to the *Financial Administration Act*, or an agency named in the schedule of this Act shall cause the department or agency to

29 S.C. 2008, c. 33.

prepare a sustainable development strategy containing objectives and plans for the department or agency that complies with and contributes to the Federal Sustainable Development Strategy, appropriate to the department or agency's mandate, and shall cause the strategy to be laid before each House of Parliament within one year after the Federal Sustainable Development Strategy is first tabled in a House of Parliament under section 10."

The Province of Quebec's *Sustainable Development Act,* also provides as follows:

7. The Government's sustainable development strategy must state the selected approach, the main issues, the directions or areas of intervention, and the objectives to be pursued by the Administration in the area of sustainable development. Where appropriate, it must also state the sustainable development principles to be taken into consideration by the Administration, in addition to those enumerated in section 6 and those set out in sections 152 and 186 of the Environment Quality Act (chapter Q-2).

For the purposes of its implementation by the Administration, the strategy must identify certain means selected to foster a concerted approach that is in keeping with all the principles of sustainable development; it must also state the roles and responsibilities of each player or certain members of the Administration in order to ensure internal efficiency and coherence. The strategy must also specify monitoring mechanisms or means.

This statement enables government to focus on priority sectors of a country and clarifies the strategy. Also, it makes a sector minister responsible for ensuring the achievement of the sustainable development goal.

## (4) Identifying the Entity or Body

Because sustainable development cuts across disciplines and ministries, its implementation requires an integrated approach, as well as a single or clearly identifiable entity to coordinate the work of the different ministries. It is vital that any sustainable development legislation identify the entity or body that is tasked with the responsibility of coordinating the implementation of the sustainable development strategy or plan, and the enforcement of the processes set out in the plan. This avoids the overlapping and duplication of functions, as well as the fractionalization of implementation that results in ineffective implementation. Section 9(1) of the Canadian federal *Sustainable Development Act* places this responsibility on the Minister. Ideally, the provision should also detail the responsibilities of the entity or body.

An example of such a detailed provision is found in the *Sustainable Development Act* of Malta (Malta's Act).[30] Malta's Act establishes the office of the Prime Minister as the competent authority for the purposes of the Act,[31] and in section 5, sets out a list of procedural obligations for the Office of the Prime Minister, including the following:

> "(a) to ensure the development and implementation of Malta's sustainable development strategy;
> (b) to revise said strategy ...
> (c) to ensure that the provisions of the strategy are implemented in a timely manner by the responsible actors;
> (d) to develop a set of indicators for measuring the progress achieved in the area of sustainable development ...;
> (h) to perform audits and to evaluate how the public administration has integrated the principles of sustainable development in its policies, plans, programs and projects;
> (l) to engage in active consultations with all stakeholders."

## (5) Statement of Principles or Overriding Policy

In the context of sustainable development, legislation that contains a statement of principles on which the sustainable development strategy is to be foundered is beneficial because it enshrines the principles in the legislation. This is essential for purposes of enforcement of the strategy. The Canadian federal legislation, as indicated above, clearly indicates that the sustainable development strategy is to be based on the precautionary principle. The *Sustainable Development Act*,[32] of the Province of Quebec, in Canada, is even

---

30 *Sustainable Development Act of Malta*, (Cap 521), Act X of 2012.
31 *Ibid.*, section 4.
32 SQ. c. D-8.1.1

more detailed with respect to setting out additional principles on which the sustainable development strategy is to be foundered, to guide the public service. It provides thusly:

"5. The implementation of sustainable development within the Administration is to be based on the sustainable development strategy adopted by the Government and is to be carried out in a manner consistent with the principles stated in the strategy and those established by this division.

6. In order to better integrate the pursuit of sustainable development into its areas of intervention, the Administration is to take the following set of principles into account when framing its actions:

(a) "*Health and quality of life*": People, human health and improved quality of life are at the centre of sustainable development concerns. People are entitled to a healthy and productive life in harmony with nature;

(b) "*Social equity and solidarity*": Development must be undertaken in a spirit of intra- and inter-generational equity and social ethics and solidarity;

(c) "*Environmental protection*": To achieve sustainable development, environmental protection must constitute an integral part of the development process;

(d) "*Economic efficiency*": The economy of Québec and its regions must be effective, geared toward innovation and economic prosperity that is conducive to social progress and respectful of the environment;

(e) "*Participation and commitment*": The participation and commitment of citizens and citizens' groups are needed to define a concerted vision of development and to ensure its environmental, social and economic sustainability;

(f) "*Access to knowledge*": Measures favourable to education, access to information and research must be encouraged in order to stimulate innovation, raise awareness and ensure effective participation of the public in the implementation of sustainable development;

(g) "*Subsidiarity*": Powers and responsibilities must be delegated to the appropriate level of authority. Decision-making centres should be adequately distributed and as close as possible to the citizens and communities concerned;

(h) *"Inter-governmental partnership and cooperation"*: Governments must collaborate to ensure that development is sustainable from an environmental, social and economic standpoint. The external impact of actions in a given territory must be taken into consideration;

(i) *"Prevention"*: In the presence of a known risk, preventive, mitigating and corrective actions must be taken, with priority given to actions at the source;

(j) *"Precaution"*: When there are threats of serious or irreversible damage, lack of full scientific certainty must not be used as a reason for postponing the adoption of effective measures to prevent environmental degradation;

(k) *"Protection of cultural heritage"*: The cultural heritage, made up of property, sites, landscapes, traditions and knowledge, reflects the identity of a society. It passes on the values of a society from generation to generation, and the preservation of this heritage fosters the sustainability of development. Cultural heritage components must be identified, protected and enhanced, taking their intrinsic rarity and fragility into account;

(l) *"Biodiversity preservation"*: Biological diversity offers incalculable advantages and must be preserved for the benefit of present and future generations. The protection of species, ecosystems and the natural processes that maintain life is essential if quality of human life is to be maintained;

(m) *"Respect for ecosystem support capacity"*: Human activities must be respectful of the support capacity of ecosystems and ensure the perenniality of ecosystems;

(n) *"Responsible production and consumption"*: Production and consumption patterns must be changed in order to make production and consumption more viable and more socially and environmentally responsible, in particular through an ecoefficient approach that avoids waste and optimizes the use of resources;

(o) *"Polluter pays"*: Those who generate pollution or whose actions otherwise degrade the environment must bear their share of the cost of measures to prevent, reduce, control and mitigate environmental damage;

(p) "*Internalization of costs*": The value of goods and services must reflect all the costs they generate for society during their whole life cycle, from their design to their final consumption and their disposal."

## (6) Monitoring and Enforcement Processes

It is crucial to the success of any sustainable development strategy or plan, that it includes a follow-up or monitoring, as well as an enforcement mechanism. The monitoring process is intended to assess the degree of success of the efforts towards attaining sustainable development goals, with a view to making changes if needed. The monitoring or follow-up process is also needed to provide an additional means of ensuring accountability. The enforcement process is intended to ensure that those persons who are given responsibilities under the strategy are held to account for their conduct.

There are two ways in which the monitoring and enforcement of the sustainable development strategy may be embodied in the legislation. First, the legislation may authorise the entity or body that is given the mandate to implement the strategy, to monitor its implementation or designate a body to do so. Second, the legislation could create a separate monitoring entity independent of the implementing entity. The same approach could apply to the process of enforcement.

The Quebec *Sustainable Development Act* is instructive in this regard. The Quebec Act provides for sustainable development evaluation and accountability mechanisms to assess advancement towards achieving the goals of sustainable development. The Act also obliges the government to develop sustainable development indicators, and appoint a Sustainable Development Commissioner who reports to the office of the Auditor General of Québec to ensure that evaluation results are transparent.

## (7) Accountability Mechanisms

A crucial component of any sustainable development legislation should be a method of holding persons, as well as public bodies that are required to undertake tasks for the advancement of sustainable development, to their obligations and promises. While review and follow-up processes introduce another level of accountability, there is the need for separate accountability mechanisms. As argued above, the absence of accountability mechanisms in current sustainable development action plans and strategies in Ghana, is one cause of their failure to advance sustainable development. Again, the Quebec Sustainable Development Act, is enlightening in this regard. It provides as follows:

> 15. In order to focus its priorities and plan its actions in a way that will foster sustainable development in keeping with the strategy of the Government, every government department and agency in the Administration must identify, in a document to be made public, the specific objectives it intends to pursue in order to contribute to a progressive and compliant implementation of the strategy, as well as the activities or interventions it plans on carrying out to that end, directly or in collaboration with one or more stakeholders in society...
>
> 17. Each government department and agency in the Administration that is subject to section 15, must state in a special section of its annual report
>
> (1) the objectives it has set in keeping with those of the strategy, in order to contribute to sustainable development and the progressive implementation of the strategy or, if applicable, the reasons why no specific objective was identified for the year given the content of the strategy adopted;
>
> (2) the various activities or interventions aimed at achieving those objectives which it successfully carried out or failed to carry out during the year, the degree to which target results were achieved, the sustainable development indicators and other monitoring mechanisms or means used; and
>
> (3) if applicable, the measures taken following comments or recommendations by the Sustainable Development Commissioner."

Under the statute, then, governmental authorities and departments are obliged to identify actions that they will take to advance the government's sustainable development strategy, and report the result of these activities on an annual basis.

## Conclusion

While most countries agree that achieving sustainable development is a worthwhile objective, and Ghana has created sustainable development strategic and actions plans, in a bid to achieve sustainable development, sustainable development has remained elusive. This paper has argued that the primary reasons for the failure of these plans are the inherent and implementation deficiencies of the plans and the absence of a legislative foundation for sustainable development. The best way to achieve sustainable development, it has been argued, is by way of legislation. The time has come for Ghana to legislate change; to use legislation to drive the implementation of sustainable development.

Legislation, this paper has argued, would force a change in attitudes by getting people to understand and accept the morality enshrined in a sustainable development conduct. As well, it would enshrine sustainable development in the country's laws by

(1) giving legal backing to the policy of sustainable development,

(2) affording priority to sustainable development across different sectors of government,

(3) increasing support for sustainable development programs and initiatives across government,

(4) granting protection to and validating sustainable development projects across government, especially environmental initiatives, and

(5) enabling the creation of indicators for the measurement of sustainable development, and the establishment of tools for monitoring and evaluating such indicators.

Drawing on examples from different jurisdictions, including Malta, Quebec, and Canada, this paper has tabled the position that the most appropriate legislation for Ghana is one that provides for a (1) statement of a purpose, (2) establishment of a process for the sustainable development plan, (3) statement of the plan's methodology, including areas of intervention, (4) identification of the entity or body that is responsible for implementing the strategy or plan, (5) statement of principles or overriding policy that will guide decision making, and (6) appropriate monitoring and enforcement procedures.